The Story of Life
From the Big Bang to You

The Story of Life

From the Big Bang to You

Kim Marshall

illustrations by
Ingrid Johnson

Holt, Rinehart and Winston / New York

Published simultaneously in Canada by Holt, Rinehart
and Winston of Canada, Limited.
Printed in the United States of America
10 9 8 7 6 5 4 3 2 1

Library of Congress Cataloging in Publication Data
Marshall, Kim. The story of life.
Summary: Presents the latest scientific theories on
the origin of the universe, the beginning of life, and
evolution of modern life forms. Also traces the development
of humans from the earliest hominids to modern civilization.
1. Evolution—Juvenile literature. 2. Life—
Origin—Juvenile literature. [1. Evolution. 2. Life—
Origin. 3. Civilization] I. Johnson, Ingrid. II. Title.
QH367.1M37 575 79-27727 ISBN 0-03-054071-2

This book is dedicated
to my mother and father,
and to my wife.
K.M.

Contents

Acknowledgments

The inspiration for this book came from several sources: J. Bronowski's television series and book *The Ascent of Man*; the *Nova* science programs on educational television; Carl Sagan's books and television appearances; Richard Leakey and Roger Lewin's book *Origins*; Stephen Jay Gould's book *Ever Since Darwin*; and the ever-present, ever-prodding curiosity of my sixth-grade students at the Martin Luther King Jr. Middle School in Boston.

I have also been stimulated and brought up-to-date by the excellent science writing in these publications: *The New York Times, Newsweek, Time, Psychology Today, Human Nature, National Geographic,* and *Harvard.* (See the Bibliography on page 154 for other sources.)

I am grateful to a number of friends and family members for encouragement and support in the seven years that this book has been in the works, especially Paul Casilli and Paula Johnson, two fellow teachers at the King School. I am deeply indebted to those who commented on earlier drafts of this book: Rudd, Lisa and Emily Crawford, Ted Dooley, Ellen and Tim Guiney, Ed, Alice, and Lynne Schneider, Ron Rosenbaum, Rosalie and Michelle Williams, Beth Ruber, Peter and Katherine Rousmaniere, Bill Perkins, Katherine Marshall, Thomas Blinkhorn, Sven Burmester, Beatrice Whitney Van Ness, Marya Levenson, George and Susan Thomas, Don and Kathryn Lombardi, Ray Pariser, John Vournakis, Eric Chaisson, Stephen Jay Gould, and my editor, Miriam Chaikin. I am also grateful to Ingrid Johnson, whose patience, hard work, and sheer talent have produced such fine illustrations for this book. Most especially I am grateful to Rhoda Schneider, my wife, whose belief in this book kept me going through thick and thin, and whose superb editing was invaluable. All these people contributed in important ways to the accuracy, accessibility, and flow of the final product.

A Note About This Book

All words printed in **boldface type** are defined in the glossary at the back of the book. If you want more detailed information on a subject, the list of books in the bibliography may help. A good library will have even more books for further research.

Most people thought the world was created and controlled by all-powerful gods. The Greeks believed in several gods, each controlling a different part of the world—the sun, the moon, lightning, the sea—and that the first human was a beautiful woman.

Introduction : *The Story of Life*

How was the Earth created? When did life begin? Where did human beings come from? For thousands of years, people have looked at the sky above them and the world around them and tried to answer these questions.

Most people came to believe that the universe was created by one or more all-powerful gods. But since each group of people saw the world in a different way, no two creation stories were the same. People around the world described their gods in very different ways, and each culture passed on a different story of life to its children. The Egyptians, the Mayan Indians, the Greeks, the Mali, the Chinese, the Hebrews, and so on—each believed in their own creation stories, usually as part of their religions.

The question is, if these stories were so different, how could they all be true? Which of the hundreds of creation stories told how the universe *really* began?

Modern scientists think that none of the early creation stories tells the complete story, but each contains a piece of the truth. Humans who lived thousands of years ago were as intelligent as we are now, but they had three disadvantages when they tried to answer questions about the origins of the universe. First, they could look at the Earth and sky only with their naked eyes, which means there was a lot they couldn't see. Second, they had little contact with people who were trying to answer the same questions in other parts of the world, which means they couldn't combine their research. And third, they had few written records of the discoveries made by people who lived before them, which means they couldn't build on those earlier discoveries but had to start from scratch most of the time.

Then, about 370 years ago, there were two very important inventions—the telescope and the microscope. One allowed people to get a much clearer look at the moon and sun and stars; the other let them see tiny objects (like germs in a drop of water) that were not visible to the naked eye. Now there was less guesswork, and people could build their theories on direct evidence and observation. They could do experiments and let others check the results. This was the beginning of the **scientific method**.

Early **scientists** peered and probed and experimented and wrote and shared their ideas. As travel became easier and more books were published, new knowledge spread from one country to another, and much of it was stored in libraries. Now each new generation of thinkers could build on the work of those who had gone before, and the growth of knowledge and discovery speeded up dramatically.

Over the years, scientists have put together a new explanation of how the universe was created and how life on Earth began. It is different from any of the creation stories of the past, and does not involve a supernatural god—although there are lots of mysterious forces and events that scientists haven't been able to explain. This book is an attempt to pull together the latest scientific theories of the story of life and present them in a brief, understandable form.

As you read, keep several things in mind. First, there are gaps in the scientific story, places where scientists haven't been able to put together a complete explanation of how things happened. Second, there are disagreements among scientists on some points, and this will be true for years to come. And third, new discoveries are being made all the time, which means that parts of this book may be outdated within a few years. No one knows the complete truth, and no book can claim to have all the answers.

But scientists do agree on the broad outlines of this new story of life, and it is being accepted by more and more people around the world. It is a story that is just as fascinating—and at times just as unbelievable—as the creation stories of old.

The beginning of our universe was an incredibly powerful explosion which scientists call the Big Bang.

1

In the Beginning

Most modern scientists believe that our universe began with a gigantic explosion that flung vast amounts of energy out into the black nothingness of space. Scientists call this the **Big Bang**, and they think it happened about 15 billion years ago.

What caused this cosmic explosion? What existed before the Big Bang? Could there have been a previous universe, with stars and planets and different forms of life? Scientists have no idea, because the Big Bang destroyed every clue. It was the birth of our universe, and we can't trace the story of life back any further than that.

Nothing but energy flew out of the Big Bang—incredible amounts of heat and radiation. In the icy temperatures of space, some of that energy condensed into matter, forming countless tiny particles. These particles eventually became stars, planets, and all living things on Earth—but that process took about 15 billion years. Let's start at the very beginning of the journey of those tiny bits of matter, from the Big Bang to you.

The First Atoms and Stars

Scientists think that shortly after the Big Bang, most of the particles flying out into space hooked together into tiny **atoms**.

These are so small that millions of them make up the period at the end of this sentence. But atoms are the building blocks of everything we see around us.

Almost all the atoms formed right after the Big Bang were **hydrogen**, the smallest and simplest atom in the universe. A few were slightly bigger atoms called **helium**. Scientists think these were the only kinds of atoms formed right after the Big Bang. There are more than a hundred kinds of atoms today, but in the beginning there were only two.

Why did the particles from the Big Bang hook together into atoms? Why didn't they keep flying out into space forever? The answer is that these particles respond to something called **electromagnetic force**, which pulls them together like little magnets. This force was at work from the beginning of the universe, for reasons that no one can explain.

Another mysterious force is **gravity**, which pulls groups of atoms together. As countless hydrogen and helium atoms flew out into space, they swirled in whirlpools and began to collect in larger and larger clouds. The larger an object is, the stronger its gravity becomes; each cloud was like a giant vacuum cleaner, pulling in more hydrogen and helium from space. The atoms they captured made them even more massive, which made their gravity even stronger, which pulled in still more atoms, and so on until each cloud was gigantic.

When anything is squeezed hard enough, it begins to heat up. Inside these giant balls, the gravity was so powerful and squeezed the atoms so hard that they began to burn. Scientists have calculated that this happens when there are about 1,000,000,000,000,000,000,000,000,000,000,000,000,000,000,000,000,000,000,000 (10 with 56 more zeros on the ends which scientists write 10^{57}) hydrogen and helium atoms pulled together in one place. These burning fireballs were the first **stars**.

Gravity pulled hydrogen and helium atoms together and squeezed them together until they heated up and began to burn. The results, in a reaction called fusion, produced a great deal of heat and light and radiation. These were burning fireballs—the first stars.

What makes a star burn? If many hydrogen atoms are squeezed and heated up enough, they begin to join into helium atoms (this reaction is called **fusion**). Groups of four hydrogen atoms form one helium atom and produce tremendous amounts of light and heat and **radiation**.

After the Big Bang, many stars were formed in this way. They swirled around in groups called **galaxies**, which took a variety of shapes. Some galaxies look like pinwheels, others like discs, others like circular clouds. Scientists estimate that there are now about 100,000,000,000 galaxies in the universe. Each galaxy has about 100,000,000,000 stars of its own, and each star has 10^{57} atoms. All this came out of the Big Bang.

Supernovas

Each star burned at very high temperatures, slowly fusing its hydrogen atoms into helium. But the biggest stars with the highest temperatures did more than this: They produced new atoms that were bigger than helium, including carbon, oxygen, nitrogen, sulphur, and iron. All atoms are basically made of the same particles (**protons**, **neutrons**, and **electrons**), but the number and way these particles are hooked together gives each kind of atom its own special properties.

The life span of a star depends on its size. Small stars burn for billions of years, and then begin to run out of hydrogen atoms. When this happens, they cool down and collapse into much smaller **white dwarfs**, which give out very little energy.

The biggest stars have much shorter lives. They get a lot hotter than small stars, burn up their hydrogen atoms more quickly, and end by collapsing inward and then exploding in what scientists call **supernovas**. Each time a supernova happens, the atoms that have been fused together inside the star are scattered into the surrounding galaxy.

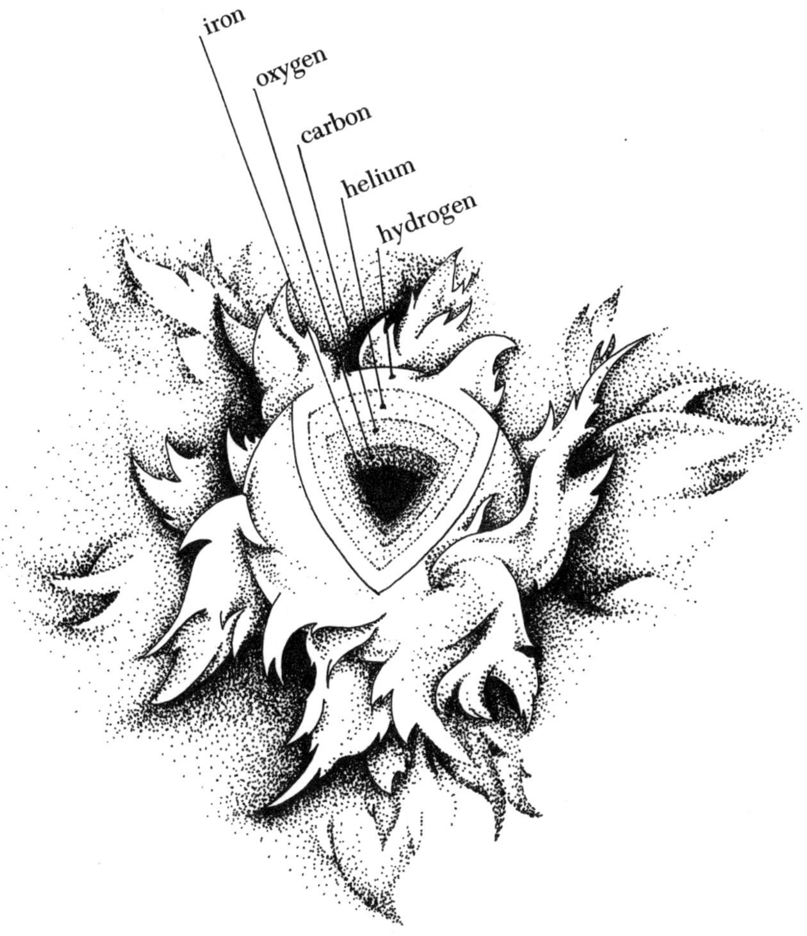

Large stars fused together many kinds of atoms. The heaviest were pulled to the center of the star, and the lightest stayed on the outside.

What's more, the heat and pressure of the supernova explosion fuses together even bigger and heavier atoms, including copper, tin, gold, uranium, and many more. Over the years, the largest stars enriched their galaxies with clouds of dust containing more than a hundred different kinds of atoms, where before

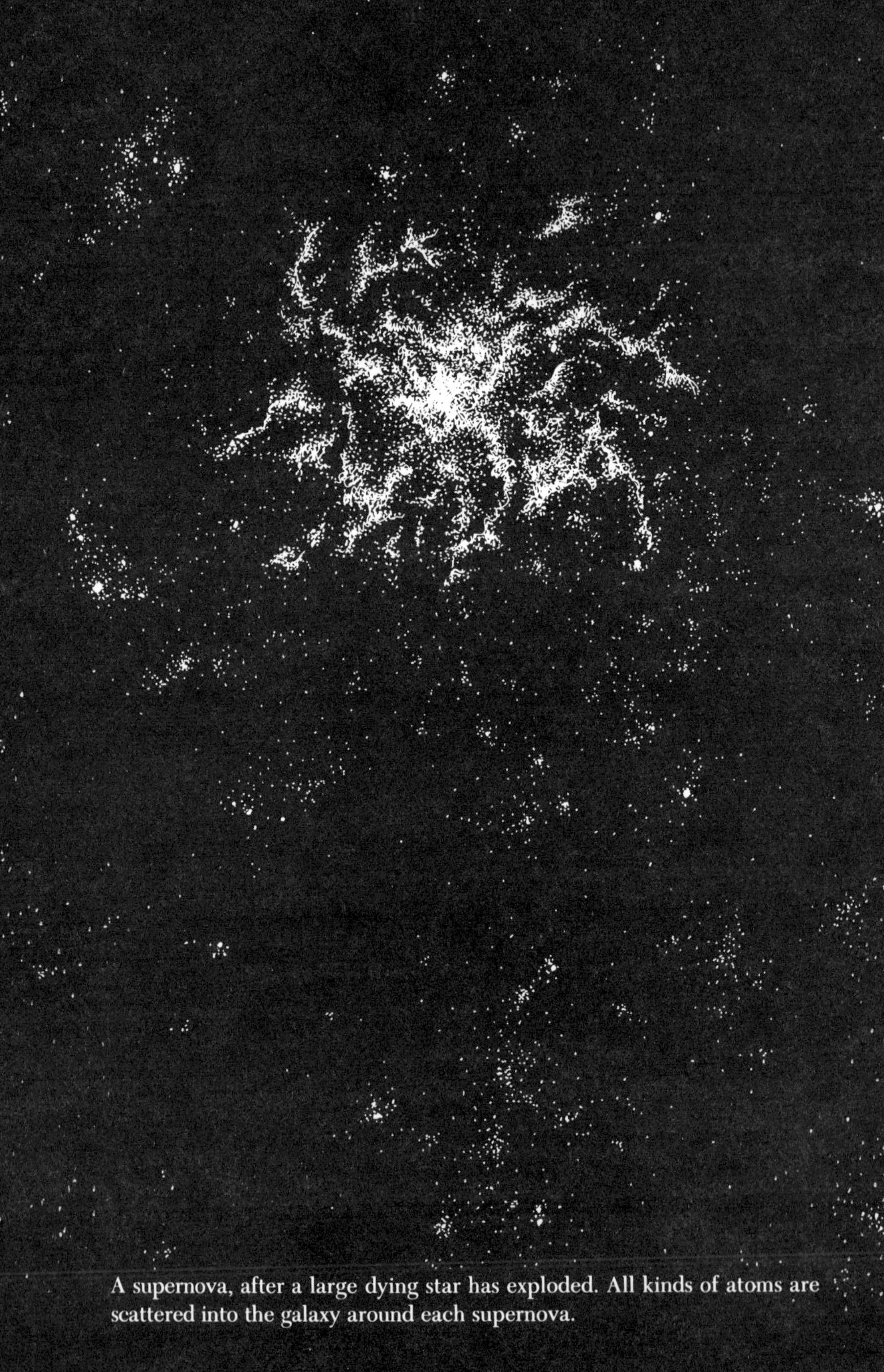

A supernova, after a large dying star has exploded. All kinds of atoms are scattered into the galaxy around each supernova.

there had been only two. This process is still going on all around the universe today.

Our Solar System

All those new atoms didn't just float aimlessly in space. They swirled into whirlpools, were pulled together into clouds by gravity, captured more atoms from space, squeezed hydrogen together, and a new generation of stars began to burn in the ancient galaxies. The difference with these new stars was that some of them had clouds of heavier atoms swirling around them. The clouds were gradually pulled together into **planets** that orbited around their local star.

One of the stars that began to burn about 5 billion years ago was our **sun**. It is in the outer reaches of a galaxy called the **Milky Way**, which was given that name because of the whitish appearance of all those billions of stars against the blackness of space. Compared to some of the giant stars of the universe, our sun is fairly small; but its size was just right for the formation of planets from the cloud of atoms around it.

By about 4½ billion years ago, the clouds had condensed into nine planets, several satellites—moons—that whirled around them, a number of smaller chunks called **meteorites**, and other chunks called **asteroids**. Each planet spun on its own **axis** and settled into its own particular orbit around the sun.

Some of the planets were far away from the sun and didn't get much of its warmth and energy. Two of the planets were close and were very hot. But the third planet out from the sun, with one moon orbiting around it, was an ideal distance away and enjoyed moderate temperatures. This was our home, the planet **Earth**.

Our sun is on the outskirts of the Milky Way galaxy, which is only one of about 100,000,000,000 galaxies in the universe.

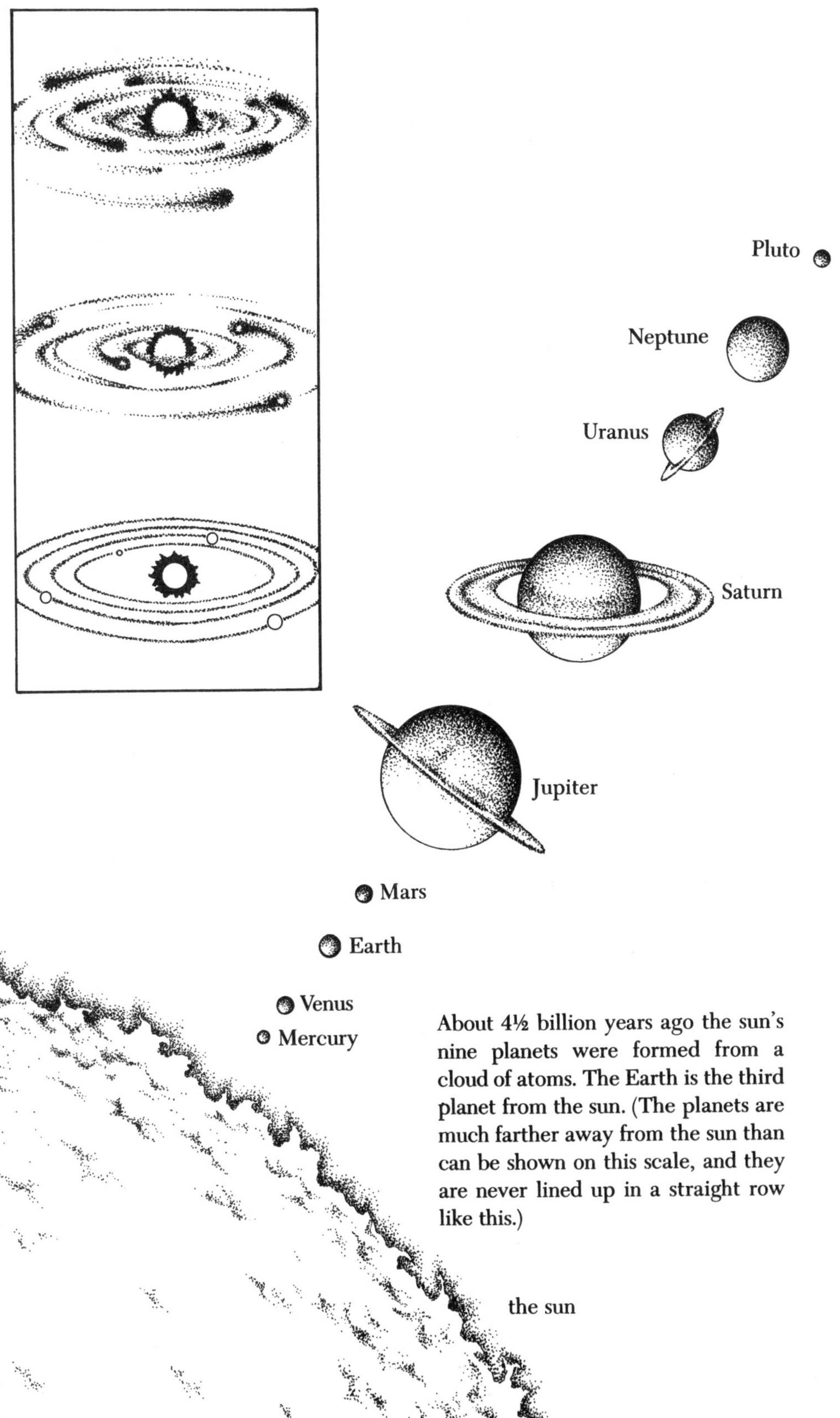

About 4½ billion years ago the sun's nine planets were formed from a cloud of atoms. The Earth is the third planet from the sun. (The planets are much farther away from the sun than can be shown on this scale, and they are never lined up in a straight row like this.)

2

The First Life

When it was first formed, the planet Earth was not a very hospitable place. There was no water and no life. Meteors were constantly crashing into it from outer space, gouging craters and sending vibrations deep into the interior.

Over the years, the Earth's radioactive atoms broke down and gave off radioactivity and heat. The young planet got hotter and hotter, until finally its core melted and became red-hot **lava**. Tons of rock and lava crunched and rumbled around, and earthquakes shuddered up to the surface.

The heat and pressure got more and more intense, and finally the red-hot lava found weak points in the Earth's crust and blasted its way through, making the first **volcanoes**. Molten lava surged to the surface, and gases that had been trapped inside the Earth spewed out into the atmosphere.

As countless atoms churned around at very high temperatures, many of them hooked together into new combinations called **molecules**. Among the new substances were several gases: water vapor (made of hydrogen and oxygen atoms), carbon dioxide (made of carbon and oxygen atoms), ammonia (hydrogen + nitrogen atoms), methane (hydrogen + carbon), and many more. A mixture of these gases hung over the pockmarked surface of the Earth. No life could exist in this scalding, corrosive atmosphere.

The First Rain

Slowly, the chemical reactions and explosions quieted down. Volcanoes erupted less often, and the surface of the Earth began to get cooler. As it did, the rocks that made up the crust cracked and buckled. This pushed up jagged mountains and cut out deep valleys.

The Earth continued to cool down. Finally the temperature on the surface was below the boiling point of water. Now water vapor in the atmosphere began to condense into clouds of little droplets, and for the first time, rain fell onto the dry, forbidding planet. It rained for many, many years. Slowly the low-lying

This cross section of the Earth shows the various layers that formed over the years. (The volcanoes and mountains do not rise so much but are drawn this way for emphasis.)

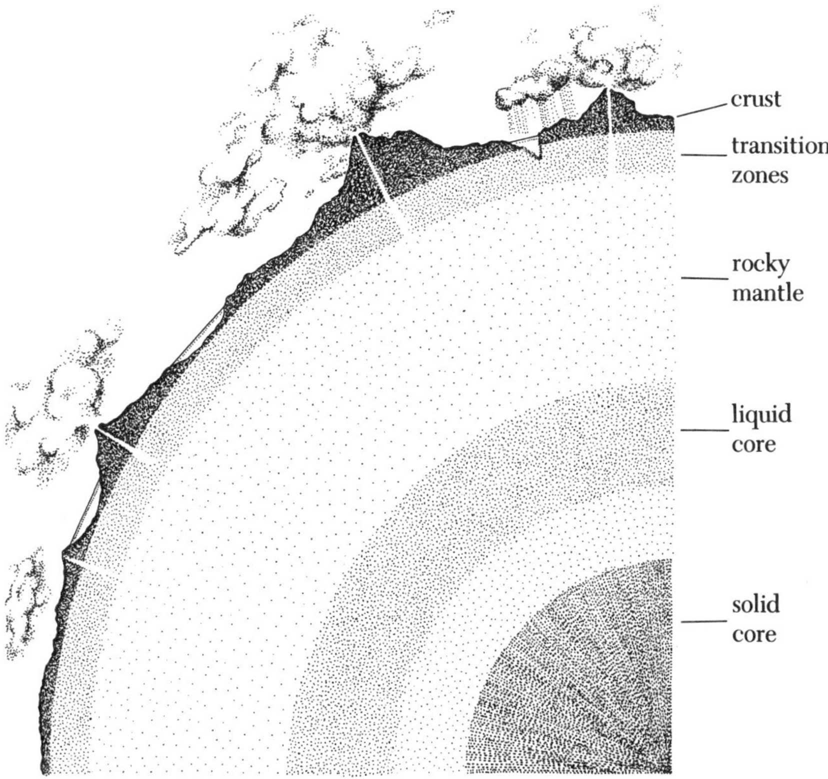

and hollow places filled up with water, and in this way the Earth's lakes and rivers and oceans were formed.

During these years of heavy rainfall, there were violent thunderstorms, with lightning bolts crashing and winds whipping up huge waves in the new oceans. As the moon orbited the Earth, its gravity pulled on the oceans, and the water began to rise and fall slightly in **tides**. Later, when the Earth had cooled down still more, ice caps formed at the north and south poles, where the sun's rays were less direct and the water froze. This trapped huge quantities of water and lowered the level of the oceans.

The drops of rain that left the clouds were fresh water. But as they fell, they dissolved some of the gases in the atmosphere and carried them down to the surface. The water that trickled over rocks and flowed along the banks of rivers dissolved other atoms and molecules and carried them down to the oceans. Over the years, the oceans became more and more "salty," a thin soup containing a mixture of hundreds of different chemicals.

Water completely changed the appearance of the Earth. From outer space, our planet now appeared mostly blue instead of gray. The pounding action of the waves in the oceans changed the shapes of many rocks, wearing away the sharp edges and making them smooth and rounded. Tiny grains of rock were carried around by ocean currents and collected as sand, mud, and clay. This process formed beaches along some coastlines, and particles of sand and dust blew onto dry land, where they began to wear away and round off and fill in the jagged landscape.

The Chemical Basis of Life

For many years, scientists couldn't figure out how the atoms and molecules on the Earth combined to make living things. Plants, fish, dinosaurs, and people are made of atoms and molecules, but they are put together in a more complicated way than the molecules in the primitive ocean. What's more, living things have energy and can reproduce, while the chemicals on the Earth 4 billion years ago were lifeless.

After years of study, scientists figured out that living things, including human bodies, are basically made of **amino acids** and **nucleotide bases**. These are molecules with millions of hydrogen, carbon, nitrogen, and oxygen atoms. How could such complicated molecules have been formed in the primitive soup? Scientists were stumped.

Then, in 1953, two scientists named Harold Urey and Stanley L. Miller did a very simple experiment to find out what had happened on the primitive Earth. They set up some tubes and bottles in a closed loop, and put in some of the same gases that were present in the atmosphere 4 billion years ago—water vapor, ammonia, carbon dioxide, methane, and hydrogen.

Then they shot an electric spark through the gases to simulate bolts of lightning on the ancient Earth, circulated the gases through some water, sent them back for more sparks, and so on. After seven days, the water that the gases had been bubbling through had turned brown. Some new chemicals were dissolved in it. When Miller and Urey analyzed the liquid, they found that it contained amino acids—the very kind of molecules found in all living things.

Word of the Miller-Urey experiment spread quickly around the world and caused great excitement. Had these two scientists solved the mystery of life? Many other scientists tried the experiment for themselves and got the same results. That meant it wasn't just a lucky accident. Some scientists altered the original experiment, and found that they could produce more amino acids *and* nucleotide bases—all the important ingredients of life. They also found that the experiment worked with other sources of energy, like **ultraviolet light** (simulating the powerful rays of the sun), heat (simulating volcanoes), **radi-**

Miller and Urey did an experiment in which they put the ingredients of the primitive Earth into some bottles and sparked them with electricity to simulate ancient thunderstorms. After seven days they had produced amino acids, one of the building blocks of life.

oactivity (simulating the energy that comes out of rocks like uranium), and shock waves (simulating earthquakes).

Since all these forms of energy were present on the primitive Earth, it seemed clear that these chemical reactions could easily have happened all by themselves 4 billion years ago. Some scientists argued that, given enough time, they *had* to happen, because all the right ingredients were there. It may have taken millions of years, but we can be sure that these life-giving molecules were produced in the ancient atmosphere and dissolved in the Earth's oceans.

Protocells

The experiments that made amino acids and nucleotide bases in bottles were very interesting, but there was just one problem: These molecules had no energy of their own. They couldn't eat or move around or reproduce. In other words, they weren't alive. The brown liquid that scientists found in their bottles may have contained chemicals found in a living body, but it was not about to crawl out of the bottle and slither across the laboratory floor.

Every living thing is made of many tiny "building blocks" called **cells**. Each cell is a growing, reproducing, living unit. Cells are made of amino acids and nucleotide bases, but inside the cell these molecules are hooked together into longer and even more complicated chemical chains called **proteins** and **nucleic acids**. Scientists realized that there were several more steps in explaining the beginning of life. Finding what these steps were has been one of the most difficult challenges faced by modern scientists. They have done thousands of experiments, and they still haven't completely figured it out. But there are some very interesting theories.

The question is how amino acids and nucleotide bases sloshing around in the primitive ocean got organized into bigger molecules and formed living cells. There were certainly many destructive forces on the primitive Earth, but what forces could have brought life out of that chemical soup?

One of the newest theories is that clay beaches at the edges of the oceans played an important part in the formation of the first cells. According to this theory, the soupy, chemical-filled ocean water was washed onto the clay beaches by the rising tide. When the tide went out, some water was left to evaporate in the sun, leaving chemicals on the clay.

Scientists simulated this process in their laboratories: They dissolved amino acids and nucleotide bases in water, poured the liquid onto some clay, and heated it with simulated sunlight until the water evaporated. Then they splashed cold water on it to simulate the next tide coming in, and lo and behold, tiny chemical bubbles were formed. They were so small that about 500 of these **microspheres** would fit on the period at the end of this sentence. When scientists analyzed them under a microscope, they found that they contained proteins like the supermolecules found in living cells. The microspheres even looked like cells. How had this happened?

The answer was that clay has a way of helping amino acids hook together into proteins, so that clay beaches naturally produced more complex molecules from the ocean water that washed up with the tides. Once again, scientists had discovered a natural process by which complicated life-giving molecules could have formed all by themselves billions of years ago. The microspheres that washed away from the clay were tiny packages of just the right supermolecules for living cells. Scientists call them **protocells**, which means that they were close to being living cells, but still lacked some vital ingredients.

The First Cells

How did these protocells get to the point where they could grow and reproduce? Scientists think that for many years, countless protocells floated around in the oceans reacting with each other and with other chemicals. Those that had the strongest skins held together, while those with weak skins were broken up by waves or by too much of the ultraviolet radiation of the sun. Only the protocells that had the right chemicals to hold together—perhaps just one in a thousand—survived.

Some of these survivors absorbed chemicals through their skins and built up bigger molecules inside. These protocells had a primitive way of "eating" the chemicals from the water around them. But as they grew larger, their skins couldn't stretch and most of them burst and were destroyed.

But a few protocells—again, maybe only one in a thousand—happened to have a different kind of skin. When they had grown to a certain point, they didn't burst, but split into smaller protocells. While others were bursting and destroying themselves, these splitting protocells survived and gradually multiplied.

Over the years, some of the surviving protocells were larger and more complex. Scientists think that by about 3½ billion years ago, there was at least one protocell that could soak up chemicals from the water, grow larger, and then split into two *identical* copies of the original. Each of these then started "eating" and growing until they in turn split in two.

These were the first living cells. Each one had received a complete message from its "parent"—EAT, GROW, SPLIT, AND PASS THIS MESSAGE ALONG. When the two new cells grew big enough, they split in two, making four cells, and all of those contained the same message and passed it along when they split in two.

Scientists call this kind of cell a **replicator**; it can make two exact copies (replicas) of itself and keep that process going in future generations. These tiny spheres in the ocean—microscopic packages of molecules that would have been invisible to the human eye—were the beginning of life on the planet Earth.

The basic process of growing by splitting in two (called **mitosis**) which the ancient protocells stumbled upon billions of years ago is still used by all forms of life today.

Cells Divide and Multiply

There had to be only one replicator to spawn trillions upon trillions of cells in the world's water and to explain all life on Earth today. Do you find that hard to believe? Try this simple arithmetic.

Suppose that among the ancient protocells only one was a replicator. It grew and split, making two exact copies of itself, each containing the same message to grow and reproduce. Now there were two living cells in the world. They followed instructions and began eating and growing until they split in two. Now the world had a population of four living cells. When they split there were eight cells. Then sixteen. Then thirty-two. Then sixty-four. The population of living cells increased very, very quickly, since every few minutes the cells split and doubled the total number.

Here's what only thirty-one generations of descendants of one original replicator would look like

first generation—1
second generation—2
third generation—4
fourth generation—8
fifth generation—16
sixth generation—32
seventh generation—64
eighth generation—128
ninth generation—256
tenth generation—512
eleventh generation—1,024

twelfth generation—2,048
thirteenth generation—4,096
fourteenth generation—8,192
fifteenth generation—16,384
sixteenth generation—32,768
seventeenth generation—65,536
eighteenth generation—131,072
nineteenth generation—262,144
twentieth generation—524,288
twenty-first generation—1,048,576
twenty-second generation—2,097,152
twenty-third generation—4,194,304
twenty-fourth generation—8,388,608
twenty-fifth generation—16,777,216
twenty-sixth generation—33,554,432
twenty-seventh generation—67,108,864
twenty-eighth generation—134,217,728
twenty-ninth generation—268,435,456
thirtieth generation—536,870,912
thirty-first generation—1,073,741,824—more than one billion cells!

This gives you some idea of how quickly the number of cells can increase when cells have the ability to split in two and pass that message along. Of course, some of those cells died or were destroyed by natural forces. But every few minutes the total population of cells on Earth doubled again. When this happened hour after hour, day after day, and year after year for millions of years, there got to be more living cells in the world's oceans than we can possibly imagine. In fact, it wasn't too long before the planet Earth experienced its first overpopulation.

3

Cells Get More Complicated

Each living cell contained the message EAT, GROW, SPLIT, AND PASS THIS MESSAGE ALONG. But how could cells understand a message? They couldn't read or write, so what form could these instructions take? For a long time this question baffled scientists, and they worked hard to figure out how the messages of life were passed from generation to generation.

Then in 1953, four scientists solved the mystery. James Watson and Francis Crick, helped by the work of Maurice Wilkins and Rosalind Franklin, figured out the structure of a super-molecule called **DNA** (short for deoxyribonucleic acid), which contained the cell messages. The three men became world famous and won the **Nobel Prize**, which is one of the highest honors a scientist can be given. But Rosalind Franklin died before people realized how important her work was, and many people feel she wasn't given the credit she deserved.

Because DNA is too small to be seen under a microscope, the scientists had to figure out how the molecules that made DNA were fitted together. They discovered that the DNA molecule looked like a twisted rope ladder, which they called a **double helix**. The "rope" and "steps" of the DNA, they said, were made of four kinds of nucleotide bases hooked together in spe-

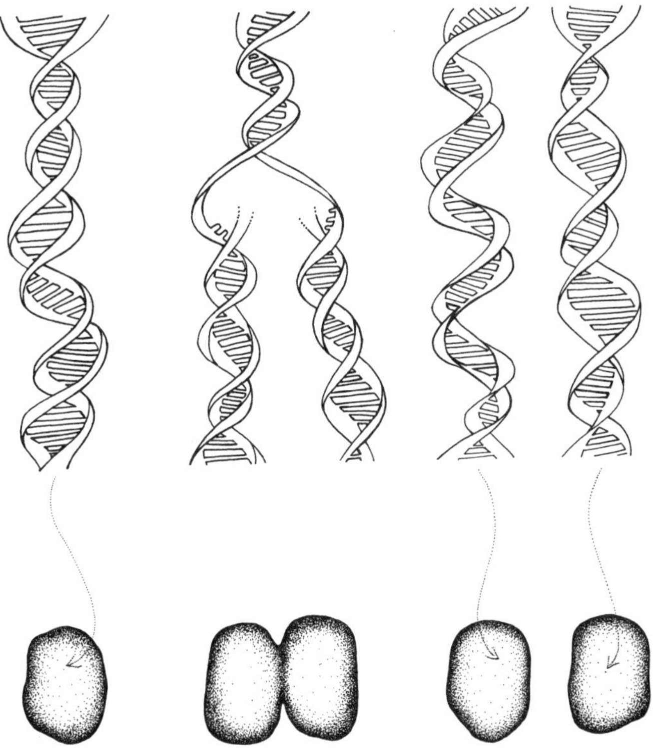

The DNA molecule inside each cell "unzips" just before the cell divides, then builds itself back to a full DNA molecule. Each new cell has a duplicate of the original DNA, with instructions to grow, split, and pass the DNA along.

cial ways that could carry the coded messages of life.

DNA is in the middle of all living cells. It acts as a memory and control center for all growth and reproduction. Each "step" in the twisted ladder is a coded "word" of instructions telling the cell how to build itself up step by step, and when to split in two.

When a cell divides, the DNA "unzips" into two strands, one for each new cell. Each DNA strand contains the full message, and immediately starts building itself back to a double helix by using the chemicals "eaten" by the cells. Soon each cell in the new generation has a full DNA molecule inside it just like the one in its parent cell. Then the process of growth and cell division starts all over again.

This remarkable ability to separate into two identical strands and build back up again is the basis for all life on Earth. Without DNA, cells would never have been able to reproduce, and the Earth's ocean would be filled with lifeless protocells today. It was a simpler version of today's DNA that gave the first living cells the ability to split and pass the message along about 3½ billion years ago, and started the amazing story of life.

Mutations

The first living cells led dangerous lives, and it's a wonder that any of them survived. Some were burned up by erupting volcanoes. Some were frozen when parts of the ocean iced over. Some were poisoned by corrosive chemicals in the water. Some were dashed to pieces by waves or electrocuted by lightning during thunderstorms. Some got too close to the surface of the water and were burned by the deadly ultraviolet rays of the sun. Some unlucky cells were washed up onto dry land and dried out amid the poison gases in the atmosphere.

But despite all these natural hazards, many cells survived and split and passed along their DNA message. Over the years, trillions upon trillions of living cells spread through the waters of the Earth.

Was every new cell exactly like its "parent"? Does DNA always make an exact copy of the original? Obviously not, because if this were true, there would be only one kind of cell on Earth today, and the oceans would be full of countless identical copies of the first living cell. But how did different kinds of cells come about?

The answer is that they were formed by accident. Most cells were exact copies of their parent cells. But every once in a while there was a mix-up in the DNA. A few chemicals got switched around and the coded message came through a little differently to the new cells, making them different from their parents. Scientists call these mistakes in the DNA **mutations** and the altered cells **mutants**.

Mutations happened all the time in the DNA of living cells, and they're still happening today. They happen more often when a cell is bombarded by strong ultraviolet light from the sun or radioactivity from certain kinds of rock. Since there was plenty of radioactivity and ultraviolet light on the ancient Earth, there were lots and lots of mutations in primitive cells as they grew and split, producing many different kinds of cells.

Most mutations didn't help cells at all. The great majority of mutants died, because their mixed-up DNA messages made them weaker and less able to hold together and they were broken up by the waves. That stopped the mixed-up DNA message right there, since there were no cells to pass it along to future generations.

But every once in a while, by sheer luck, mutations produced a new combination of DNA messages that didn't get the mutants killed. In some cases the accidental DNA instructions made mutants better able to survive in the primitive ocean. Say a new DNA message made the mutant cells thicker skinned or green colored. These mutants survived, reproduced, and passed on their new DNA message to future generations. What started as random mistakes led to new branches of living cells, in this case whole families of green-colored or thicker-skinned cells.

Over the years, most of the mutations were the bad kind that weakened and killed the mutants. But those one-in-a-million good mutations were passed along to future generations of survivors, and produced a great variety of cells. Soon there were many different shapes and sizes and colors of cells floating around in the water.

Evolution

After millions of years of reproduction, the cells growing in many parts of the Earth began to have a population problem. There wasn't enough chemical food in the water to go around. This meant that some cells had to die of starvation. The question is, which cells would survive?

This is where a process called **natural selection** began. Of all the different kinds of cells living in a particular overcrowded place, only those that were best adapted to that place survived. Those that were less adapted to the heat or the cold or the chemicals of that environment were the first to die when food was short.

It was a three-step process: Mutations produced a great variety of cells; reproduction produced a great number of cells until there were too many for all of them to survive; and by natural selection those that fit best into a certain environment survived. After many generations of natural selection, the survivors were much better adapted to their surroundings than their ancestors had been. This gradual process of change in living things is called **evolution**.

Bacteria and Algae

Most cells "ate" chemicals from the water around them. But some mutant cells were able to "eat" other living cells. These cell eaters had a great advantage over other cells: Even when chemical food was scarce, they were able to survive and reproduce. Their DNA code said EAT CELLS, GROW, SPLIT, AND PASS THIS MESSAGE ALONG. They were the ancestors of modern **bacteria** cells (germs), which survive in much the same way today. In overcrowded parts of the primitive ocean, bacteria were very well adapted, and soon there were trillions upon trillions of them munching away on the cells around them.

About 3.3 billion years ago, mutations also produced new

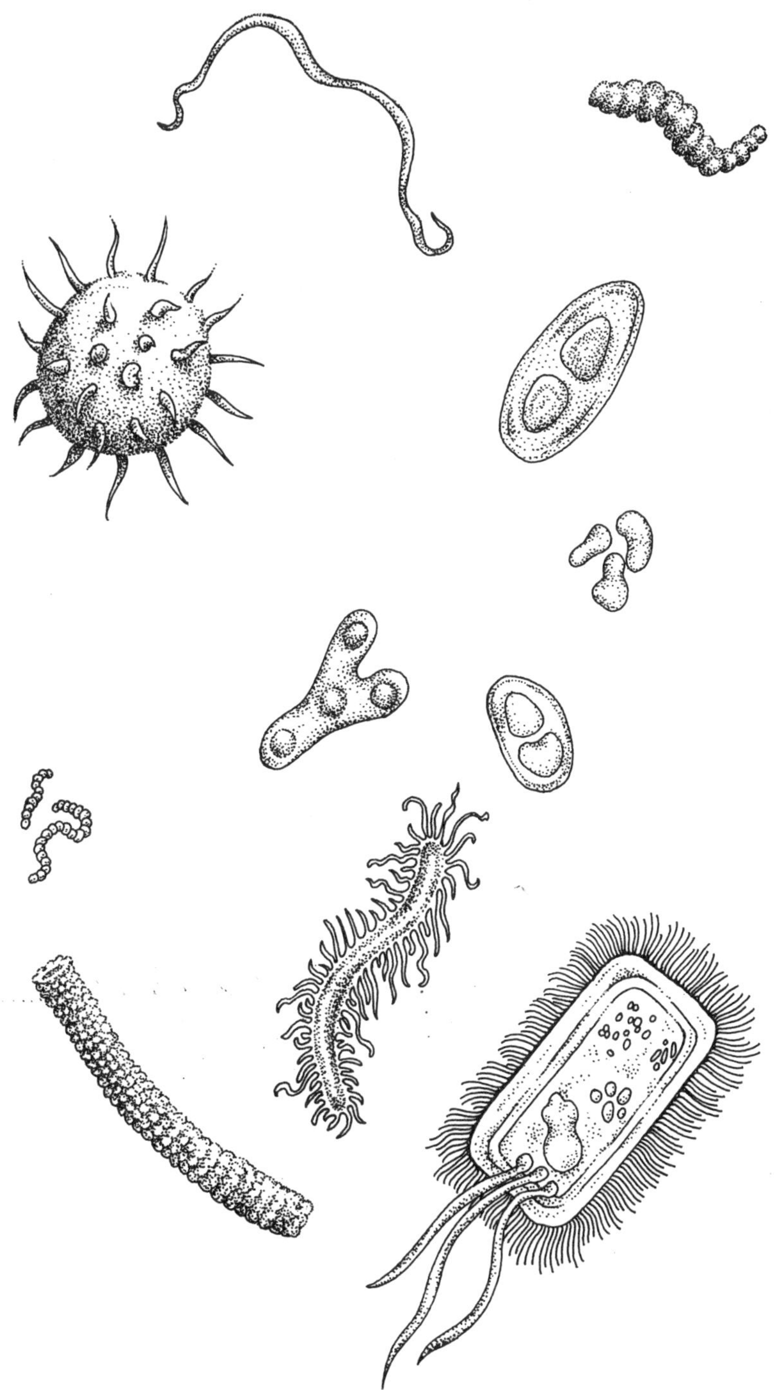

These are greatly magnified drawings of some bacteria and virus cells.

green-colored cells which had yet another way of surviving the food shortage. These cells had a chemical, **chlorophyll**, inside, which soaked up the rays of the sun and used that energy to make protein—food—for the cell. The new green cells didn't need to eat chemicals from the water; all they needed was sunlight, water, and carbon dioxide gas and they could grow and reproduce forever. The chemical reaction inside these green cells is called **photosynthesis**, which comes from Latin words meaning "to make something out of light."

With chemical food running low in the overcrowded parts of the Earth, these "sunlight-eating" cells had stumbled on an excellent way to survive. There was no shortage of sunlight, water, and carbon dioxide, so the green cells multiplied and spread rapidly. Soon there were many, many green cells floating around in the Earth's oceans, rivers, lakes, and ponds.

Later, these cells grew together in colonies and formed thick mats. Scientists have found the dried-up, hardened remains of some of these mats and called them **stromatolites**. By looking at them through microscopes, scientists have found that these ancient green cells were the direct ancestors of the blue-green algae that you can find today in rivers, lakes, and some swimming pools.

Oxygen

There was just one problem with this new form of cell: The chemical reaction inside each one bubbled out oxygen gas. We are used to thinking of oxygen as necessary to life, but billions of years ago the very opposite was true: Oxygen was a deadly poison. Before green cells evolved, all the Earth's oxygen was hooked into molecules such as water (H_2O) and carbon dioxide (CO_2). When free (unhooked) oxygen bubbled out of the green algae cells, it started reactions in most primitive cells that killed them. Cells had evolved in an environment with no free oxygen, and they were not equipped to live with it. Now cells that had been well adapted to their environment were suddenly not well adapted at all.

As more and more of the deadly gas dissolved in the water, it poisoned and killed countless primitive cells. Out of all the different kinds of cells that had been produced by mutations, which ones would survive in the new environment?

Some bacteria cells grew and reproduced under the mud at the bottom of the water. When oxygen began to fill the water, they had a great advantage, because the oxygen couldn't reach them. They survived, and passed on a DNA message that said EAT CELLS, GROW, SPLIT, STAY IN THE MUD, AND PASS THIS MESSAGE ALONG. There are still many kinds of bacteria like this today, and they still live only in places with no oxygen and die in the open air.

A second kind of cell that was able to survive were those with oxygen-proof skins—which included the green cells themselves. These cells soaked up their regular chemical food or carbon dioxide but were somehow able to keep oxygen out. They grew and multiplied in the water even with the poisonous oxygen all around them.

A third way of surviving the presence of oxygen was to soak up oxygen and use it to make food. This may sound odd, "eating" something that was poisonous, but a few primitive mutants had chemical reactions inside them that allowed them to combine oxygen with other molecules in a way that helped them to grow. In fact, the new oxygen-using cells could grow and reproduce much more quickly than either bacteria or algae cells, so they spread quickly in ancient waters. The oxygen-using cells bubbled out a waste product of their own—carbon dioxide—which happened to be one of the things the algae cells needed. These two kinds of cells helped each other survive.

By bubbling out oxygen, the green algae cells caused the

death of countless primitive cells. The presence of oxygen completely changed the conditions of life underwater, and only cells that lived in the mud, kept oxygen out, or used oxygen in new chemical reactions could survive. After a while, almost all cells could live with oxygen around. It was no longer a poisonous gas; it was just part of the new underwater environment to which all living cells had adapted. Those that weren't adapted were no longer part of the continuing story of life.

A New Atmosphere

Oxygen also changed the atmosphere above the surface of the Earth. Before the green cells got going, there were only methane, ammonia, carbon dioxide, and other gases around the planet. But the little bubbles coming out of the underwater algae floated up to the top of the water and out into the atmosphere. As countless algae cells bubbled year after year, oxygen took up an increasing part of the layer of gases around the Earth. Today oxygen makes up one fifth of the atmosphere, and most of it came from those tiny algae cells in the ancient oceans.

Oxygen had one more important effect above the Earth. Many of the oxygen atoms formed a new gas called **ozone** (made of three oxygen atoms hooked together). Ozone floated in a layer about 30 miles above the Earth. This ozone layer had a way of filtering out most of the deadly ultraviolet rays of the sun. As the layer got thicker, the sunlight that reached the Earth was less destructive to life. For the first time, cells could survive close to the surface of the water.

Modern Cells

For many, many years, the story of life on Earth was the story of tiny changes inside tiny cells. The basic chemicals didn't change much—amino acids and nucleotide bases, proteins and DNA—but the DNA messages got more complicated as cells

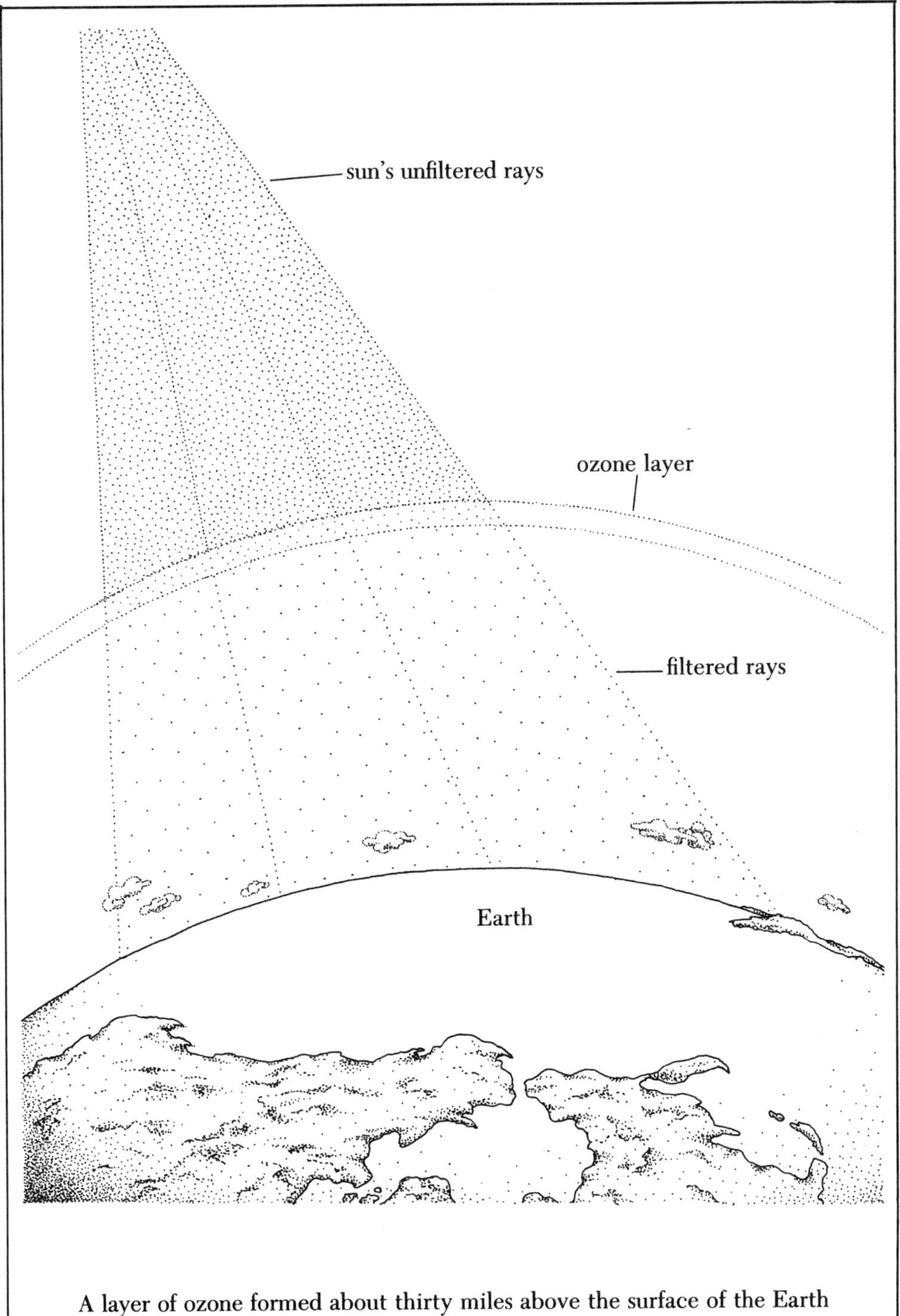

A layer of ozone formed about thirty miles above the surface of the Earth and filtered out most of the harmful ultraviolet rays of the sun. (Note: This drawing is not to scale.)

evolved in ways that fit into different environments and mutations produced more variety.

By about 2 billion years ago, the most complicated cells were **eucaryotes**, which were very similar to the cells in all living things today. The DNA of these eucaryotes was wrapped in a control center in the middle of the cell called a **nucleus**. Some eucaryotes had green blobs (**chloroplasts**) inside, which allowed them to make their food from sunlight, just like the ancient algae cells. These were the ancestors of all modern plants.

Other eucaryotes had little subcells (**mitochondria**) inside, which allowed them to use oxygen to make their food, just like the ancient oxygen-using cells. They also had little spinners (**flagella**) attached to the outside that moved them around the way outboard motors move speedboats. These mobile cells were the ancestors of all modern animals.

No one knows just how these eucaryotic cells evolved; that is one of the gaps in the scientific story of life. Scientists know that eucaryotes evolved from primitive cells, and that somehow the sunlight-using and oxygen-using parts entered larger cells and stayed as permanent guests. But the exact way that this happened is still a mystery.

What is clear is that from the time eucaryotic cells first evolved, the plant and animal cells couldn't live without each other. Plant cells needed the carbon dioxide that the animal cells were bubbling out, and animal cells needed the oxygen that the plant cells bubbled out.

If there had been nothing but plant cells in the water, they would have used up all the carbon dioxide and died out. If there had been nothing but animal cells, they would have used up all the oxygen and died out. As it was, these two branches of life balanced each other perfectly, each producing what the other needed. And over the years they both thrived in the water, growing and multiplying and mutating and spreading and evolving and forever passing the message along.

4

Plants and Animals

For a long time, the only way cells could reproduce was by splitting in two. But by about 1 billion years ago, a new way of passing the DNA messages to the next generation had evolved—sexual reproduction. Here's how it worked: Two parent cells joined together for a few moments and combined special single strands of their DNA, one from each parent. The new DNA had different messages from each parent, and started the growth of a new cell that was different from either one of them.

With sexual reproduction, it took two cells to make one new one, so it was slower than mitosis. But there was one very important advantage: No two cells made this way were the same. Each one had a new DNA message that combined some messages from its "mother" and some from its "father." Sexual reproduction produced much more variety in living things, which greatly speeded up the pace of evolution.

There were still plenty of bacteria, algae, and other simple cells that reproduced by splitting in two. These microscopic cells stayed almost the same over the years, changed only by an occasional mutation. But sexually reproducing plant and animal cells evolved into much larger and more complex forms of life.

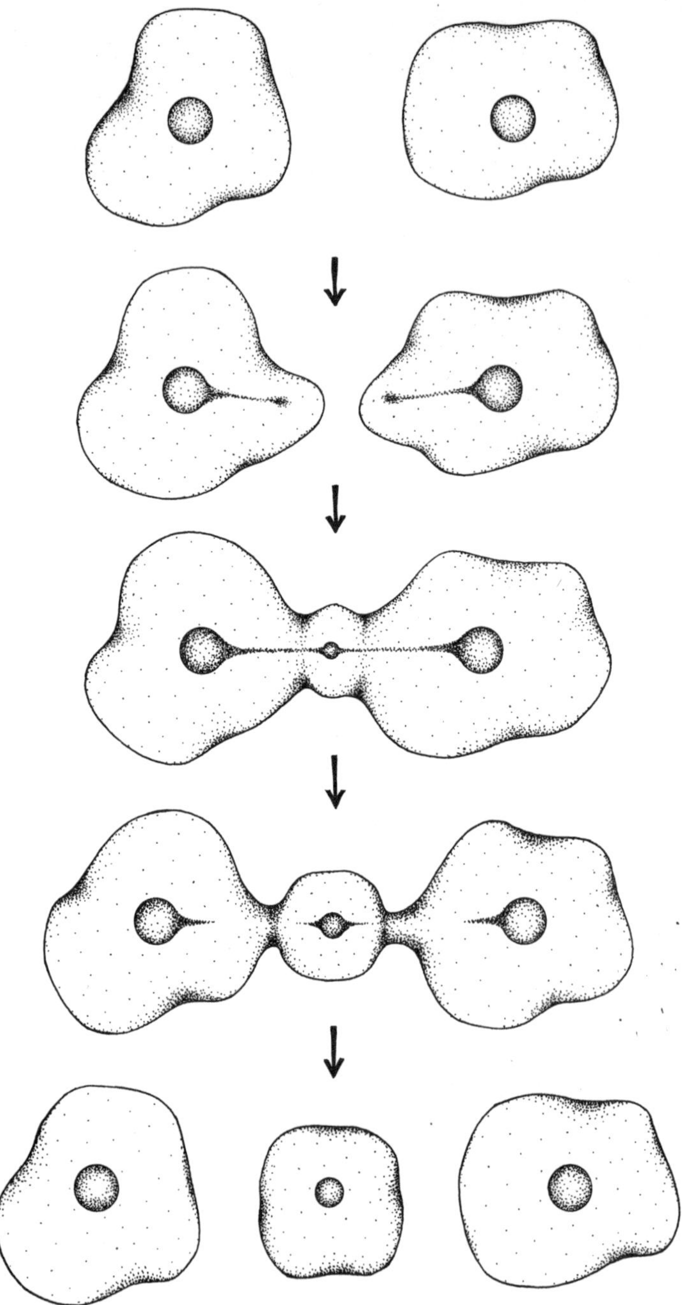

Two sexually reproducing cells (greatly enlarged here) combine their DNAs to make a new cell.

Organisms

At some point more than 1 billion years ago, some cells began growing together in large colonies, like the algae stromatolites mentioned earlier. This happened because there were mutations that gave some cells sticky skins so that they clung to the cells around them. A colony of cells was less likely than a single cell to be broken up by waves and other natural forces. United, they were stronger, and so the mutant cells with sticky skins survived, multiplied, and passed their stickiness down through the generations. (EAT, GROW, STICK TOGETHER, SPLIT, AND PASS THIS MESSAGE ALONG.) Large colonies of cells became fairly common in the primitive ocean.

Millions of years later, some of these colonies had evolved into the first **organisms**—organized teams of cells that were the first real plants and animals. Scientists don't yet understand how this happened, but different cells had evolved so that they did different jobs in the organism. In plants, some cells grew into stems, some into branches, some into leaves, and so on. In animals, some cells grew into feelers, some into legs, some into skin, and so on. Plant and animal organisms were directed by a much more complicated DNA message, which was like an architect's drawing for building the whole body.

Organisms had important advantages over single cells and colonies of identical cells. By working as a team with specializing members, the plant or animal cells could better protect themselves from the dangers in the water, and could get more of the food they needed. Many of the new plants and animals survived and reproduced, and with each new generation there were new combinations of the DNA—which, along with mutations, produced an amazing variety of plants and animals. By about 600 million years ago, there were plants of all different sizes and colors and shapes, each with its own way of catching the rays of the sun to grow and survive. And there were numer-

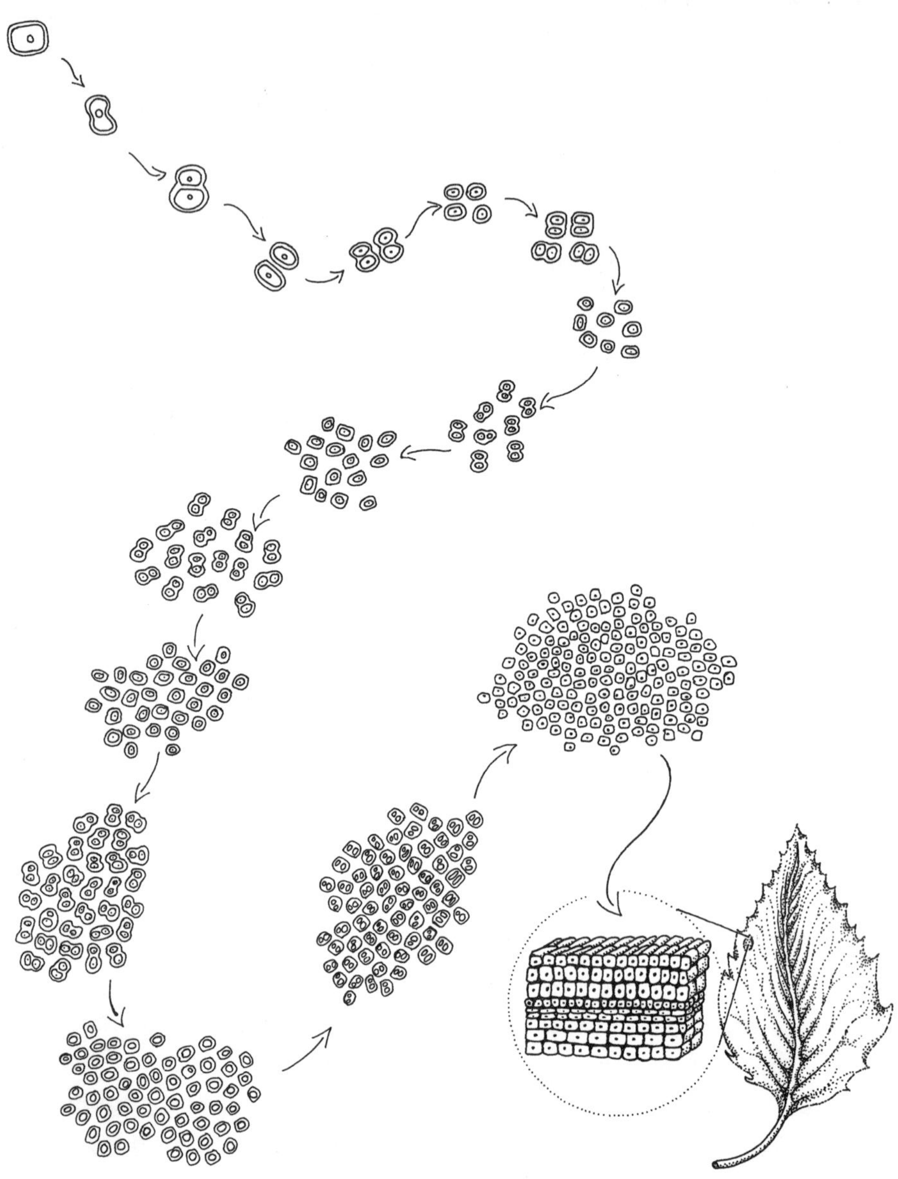

Cell division as an organism grows from the top single cell. Every organism starts with one cell, splits into two, then into four, then into eight, then into sixteen, and so forth. The cells shown here have instructions in their DNA to form part of a leaf in a tree.

ous primitive animals, including jellyfish, which got their food by floating parts of their bodies out to catch nutrients; sponges, which soaked up water and ate the nutrients in it; and coral and sea anemones, which sat on the bottom and ate bits of protein that sank nearby.

There were also starfish, primitive worms, and other large animals. Each had as many as a billion cells, all coordinated to move the body around, avoid danger, find food, and reproduce. Worms had a new way of digesting the protein they ate: They pulled their food in at one end, soaked up the protein inside a tube through the middle of their body (the **gut**), and pushed the waste out the other end.

A primitive worm, with a cross section showing the gut through which food passes. The worm digests the nutrients in the food here before pushing the waste products out the other end.

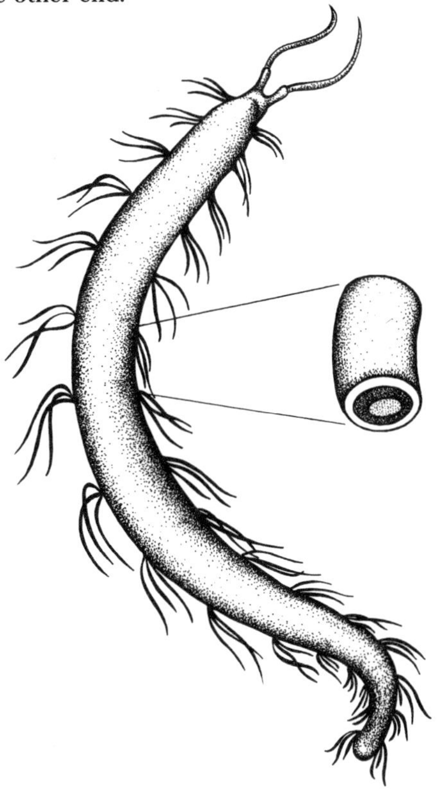

Now that there were so many different kinds of organisms in the ocean reproducing sexually, there is an obvious question: Could a starfish reproduce with a worm? Could a sea anemone reproduce with a sponge? The answer is no. The reason is that these animals had evolved in such different ways that their DNAs would not hook together. Animals and plants reproduce only with other members of their **species**. Their DNA has instructions allowing them to reproduce only with similar organisms.

Invertebrates

As more and more species of animals evolved and chomped away on the available food supply and reproduced, a familiar problem arose: Some areas became too crowded, and there wasn't enough food to go around. So animals turned to other animals for food, which was a good idea since living bodies were all basically made of protein and were nutritious meals.

Animals that eat other animals are called **predators**. They became one of the environmental hazards that affected the evolution of many living things. Any plant or animal that was always getting eaten by predators was in serious danger of becoming **extinct** (dying out completely). Species of plants and animals could survive only if their members had ways to keep from being eaten.

Years of DNA changes and mutations produced many adaptations that helped living things survive. Some animals, like the snail, **scorpion**, and **trilobite**, evolved with hard shells protecting their soft bodies from harm. (These animals are called **invertebrates**, which means they didn't have internal skeletons or backbones.) Some animals, like the **sea urchin**, had sharp spines to keep predators away. Some, like the starfish, camouflaged themselves or hid from predators. Some plants and animals tasted bad, so predators wouldn't want to eat the protein in

An imaginary scene showing various plants, a starfish, a trilobite, a jellyfish, and a cephalopod—a squidlike animal—underwater about 700 million years ago.

their bodies. And some animals moved so fast that predators couldn't catch them. These were often predators themselves.

How do we know about all these different kinds of animals living underwater hundreds of millions of years ago? Most soft-bodied animals rotted away when they died, leaving few lasting traces. But many hard-shelled invertebrates left **fossils** in ancient rocks, which scientists have been able to examine closely. Here's how a fossil is formed: Let's say that a snail is buried in mud after it dies. The mud dries out and hardens into rock over the years, and the shell of the snail is preserved or slowly replaced by rock, leaving a clear imprint in the rock—a fossil. Since scientists can accurately tell how old a rock is, they can figure out exactly what kinds of life were thriving in the ocean at what times.

The First Fish

Some species of worms evolved with little legs that moved them along and feelers that told them what was going on around them. After millions more years of mutations and DNA changes, some species had evolved with fins and muscles and tough material called **cartilage** inside them to hold their bigger bodies together. These were the first fish. Modern sharks are built along the same lines, except that these early fish did not have movable jaws.

After many more millions of years of gradual evolution, some fish had backbones and skeletons of hard bones. (Animals with backbones and internal skeletons are called **vertebrates**.) The fossils of the first bony creatures have been found in rocks dating back around 440 million years. Over the next few million years, many different species of fish evolved.

Like other animals, fish had to compete for their food, but they had a great advantage over soft-bodied animals and invertebrates: Fish were much faster and stronger. The main com-

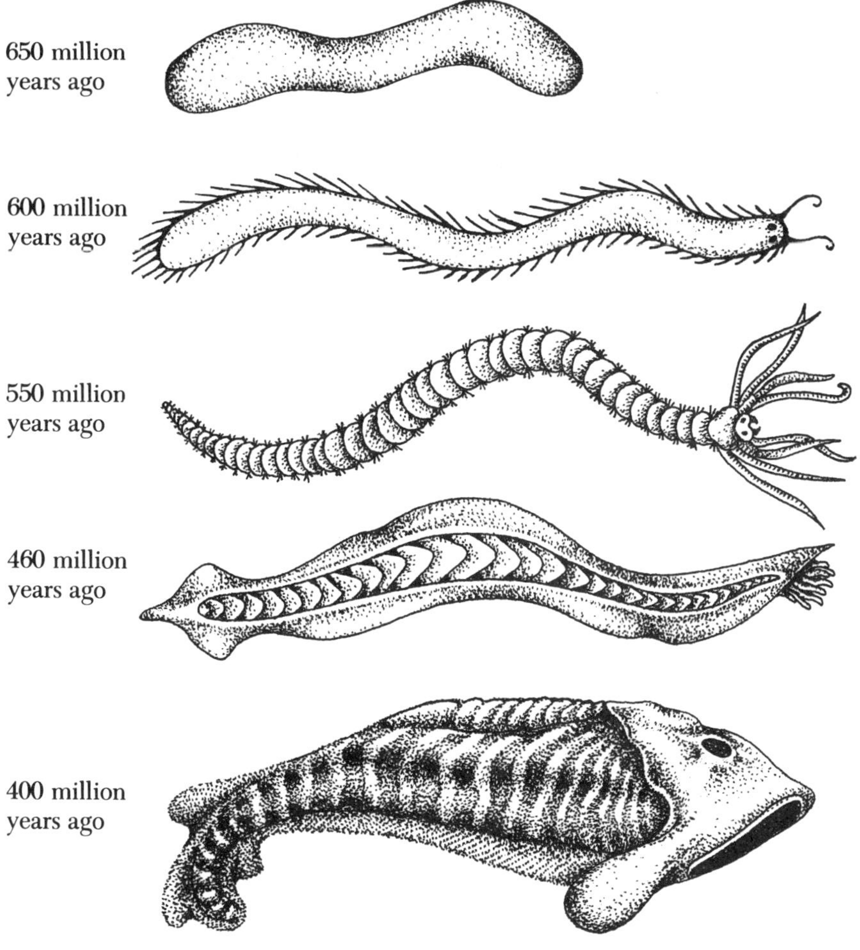

It took millions of years of mutations and DNA changes for the worm to evolve to the jawless fish.

petition came from other fish, and natural selection favored the fastest and strongest and best adapted. Those fish that could not get food or protect themselves became extinct.

By about 400 million years ago, the best-adapted fish had very complicated bodies. They had eyes and other sense organs to warn them of danger and help them find food. They had muscles attached to their bones to move them around in the water. They had brains that sent and received signals to and from all parts of their bodies through nerve cells. They had pumping hearts and tubes that carried blood to keep body cells alive, and gills to pull oxygen out of the water and bring it to the blood. They had guts to digest their food, kidneys to filter the blood, and livers to regulate chemicals around the body.

They also had a unique way of combining the DNA in their sex cells with the DNA of another fish. Over the years, two different sexes had evolved. A female fish spread her tiny egg cells, each containing a single strand of her DNA, on the bottom of the ocean or pond or river. Then the male fish spread his sex cells (**sperm**, each of which contained a single strand of his DNA) over the eggs. The male and female cells hooked together, their DNAs joined (that's the moment of **fertilization**), and each cell started to grow into a new fish.

Every fish (and every other animal and plant that reproduced sexually) started as just one fertilized cell, with all the instructions for making the complete body encoded in its DNA. (The DNA message of a fish was so long that it would fill several books if it could be written out. But even that complicated DNA strand is too small to be seen under a microscope.) The cell split into two, then into four, then into eight, then into sixteen, and so on.

But unlike primitive single-cell life, which kept making copies of the original, these cells began to develop into different parts of the fish's body: Some grew into muscle, some into bones, some into the heart, some into blood, some into the brain, some into fins, and some into special sex cells (these separated the DNA into single strands in a process called **meiosis**). Finally, the complete organism was ready to swim around, eat, grow, and produce another generation of fish.

The Move to Dry Land

While all this evolution was going on underwater, the Earth's dry land continued to be a barren wasteland. But the presence of oxygen and the ozone layer made life possible in the air. How did living things start to live out of the water? As you might expect, it happened as a result of a series of accidental events.

Many kinds of plants thrived under shallow water in lakes, ponds, and swamps around the world. Some were thin and delicate, others were short and thick skinned; some floated on the surface while others rooted themselves to the bottom. But then some of these areas of shallow water dried up (perhaps because of earthquakes or an overly hot climate). The plants that were adapted to an underwater environment were suddenly high and dry, and most of them died.

But a few plants happened to have adaptations (thick skin to keep moisture in, roots to pull water up from underground) that helped them survive. If there was plenty of rain, these hardy plants managed to make it on dry land, passing on their special adaptations to future generations. The early land-dwelling plants gradually evolved, and their descendants were better adapted to the new environment. Various kinds of plants spread slowly over the Earth, adapting to everything from the swamps to the deserts and the barren slopes of mountains.

(When they died, plants rotted and the chemicals in their remains acted as fertilizer for growing plants. Over the years, many rotting plants were buried and squeezed and chemically changed until they became coal or thick black oil.)

After plants began to live on dry land, some animals made the move. In some places, it probably happened in much the same way it had for plants: A few underwater animals left high and dry happened to have bodies that could survive out of the water. But there is a big difference between plants and animals: Animals can usually move around in search of food, while

Plant life begins to grow on dry land. The plants that are adapted to living on land survive, while those that are not adapted dry up and die.

plants usually stay still and soak up the rays of the sun. There may have been underwater animals that crawled out of the water in search of food. Any animal that could do this had a great survival advantage, because there was so much plant life to eat on land, and so little competition from other animals.

The first land-dwelling animals were probably small invertebrates like trilobites and scorpions whose shells could hold in the moisture. For a while they enjoyed a perfect environment, and they grew and reproduced and passed along their special land-dwelling adaptations. Over the years there were more mutations and DNA changes, and many different species of land animals evolved—earthworms, spiders, insects, among others—and spread around to different environments. Before long, dry land was teeming with little animals, and they were competing with each other for the plant food that had once been so plentiful. A good thing never seems to last for very long.

5

Amphibians and Reptiles

It took millions of years of gradual evolution before plants and invertebrates could live on dry land. It took vertebrates even longer. Fish were poorly adapted to living out of the water. Their bodies and fins were made for swimming, not crawling. Their gills could pull dissolved oxygen from the water into their lungs, but were of no use for breathing air directly. If fish were washed up on land by storms or left high and dry when a pond evaporated, they didn't live very long.

But in some shallow, stagnant ponds where swimming was difficult and there wasn't much oxygen in the water, new species of fish evolved. They had bonier fins and the ability to gulp in fresh air. Other fish in these stagnant ponds died, but the new species survived. Their better-adapted bodies allowed them to scuttle along the bottom and come up for air when there wasn't enough oxygen in the water.

Many years later, some of the bony-finned, air-breathing fish were good enough at crawling so that if they were stranded out of the water, they could flop along the land to another pond. Some of them may even have crawled out of their home ponds to others nearby where there was more food and less competition from other fish.

After many more mutations and gradual DNA changes, the

best-adapted survivors were able to spend more time out of the water, taking advantage of the ample supply of food on land. As they began to compete with each other for food, those that were best adapted survived and passed on their adaptations to

These drawings show the gradual evolution from the jawless fish to the first amphibians.

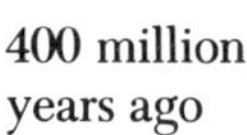
400 million years ago

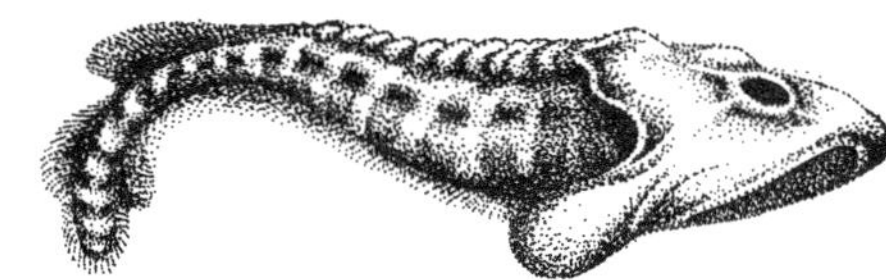

380 million years ago

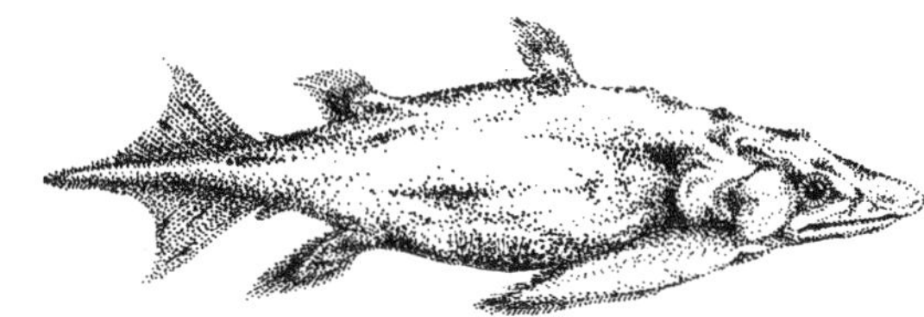

360 million years ago

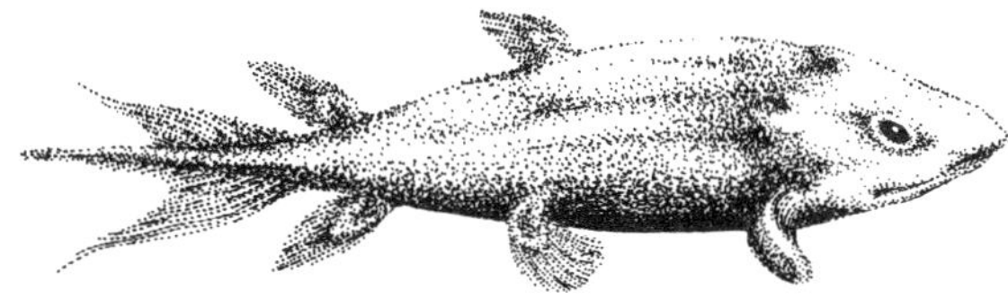

350 million years ago

340 million years ago

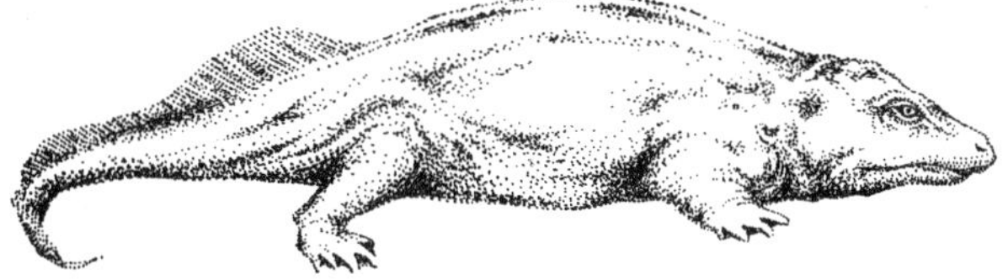

their young. These creatures that spent part of their time in the water and part on dry land were the first **amphibians**. Fossils indicate that they evolved about 340 million years ago.

Tougher Eggs

The first amphibians reproduced in the same way as their cousins the fish: Females laid their soft eggs in the water, and males fertilized them with their sperm cells so the eggs could start growing into a new generation of amphibians. If an amphibian made the mistake of laying her eggs on land, the eggs dried out and none of them hatched and lived. The surviving amphibians had instincts in their DNA and their small brains that told them to look for their food on land and do their mating in the water.

Amphibians gradually spread out to different parts of the world, and many species evolved. Some were small and nimble, feeding on the crawling and flying insects and the plants that lived on dry land. Other amphibians were bigger, thicker skinned, and fiercer, and competed with other large amphibians for a limited food supply.

Because they were often up on land looking for food, amphibians had a problem: The eggs they left behind in the water were often eaten by fish. This was a threat to the survival of amphibians, since a species couldn't live on unless a certain percentage of eggs hatched.

Many species may have become extinct as fish ate their eggs, but a few amphibians had mutations which made eggs with thicker skins. These eggs were harder for fish to eat, and had a better chance of hatching and surviving. They passed along the DNA code for thicker egg skins to future generations. Over the years, many amphibians with soft eggs died out, and those that laid thick-skinned eggs survived.

But what about mating? Could the amphibians that laid harder-skinned eggs combine their DNA in the same way as

Amphibians got most of their food on dry land, but they still mated and hatched their eggs underwater.

early amphibians and fish? The answer is no; if the male squirted his sperm cells over these eggs, the sperm couldn't get through the skin to fertilize them. A different system was needed for these amphibians to survive.

As harder-skinned eggs evolved, so also did a new system of mating and fertilization. Males squirted their sperm cells into the female's body *before* she laid her eggs, fertilizing them before the hard shell was formed. When the eggs were laid, they were ready to grow on their own, with no more help from the male.

Reptiles

During the time amphibians were spreading over the Earth, the surface of our planet was being rearranged by powerful forces from its red-hot interior. All the land masses were slowly pushed together until they formed one massive continent—**Pangaea**. As the land masses crunched together, a lot of the warm, shallow seas were dried up, and many forms of underwater animals were killed and became extinct.

At the time Pangaea was formed, the Earth's climate became hotter and drier. The water in many swamps and lakes where amphibians lived evaporated. Many amphibians were forced to spend more and more time on dry land and even had to lay their eggs out of the water. In the hottest and driest parts of the world, millions of amphibians died, and only the few that happened to have thicker skin and harder eggshells to keep the moisture inside were able to survive. These fortunate few passed their new land-dwelling adaptations along to future generations. After many years of further evolution, new species of vertebrates were spending all their time on dry land and were fully adapted to the new environment. These were the first **reptiles**. They probably looked a little like modern lizards. Very few amphibians survived this period of dry climate.

Among those that did were the ancestors of modern frogs and toads.

At this point, reptiles were the biggest, strongest, and hungriest creatures on Earth. They reproduced and spread quickly, and before long there were many species living in many different environments around Pangaea—grasslands, mountains, deserts, and so on. Among the kinds of reptiles were turtles, snakes, crocodiles, flying pterodactyls, and, largest of all, dinosaurs. These reptiles may have been very different in appearance, but they all used the same basic method of reproduction: combining the male and female DNA inside the mother's body and then laying fertilized tough-shelled eggs to hatch on dry land.

Like fish and other early forms of life, reptiles were **cold-blooded.** This means that their body temperature was the same as the temperature of the air or water around them. It went down when the weather was cold and up when it was hot. The problem with being cold-blooded on land was that air temperature varies more than water temperature. When the air got chilly (at night or in the winter), reptiles' bodies slowed down and became very sluggish. These creatures needed warm weather to move around, get their food, and survive.

Fortunately for them, reptiles evolved at the beginning of a long period of warm weather. The temperature stayed high during the day, lush green vegetation spread to most of Pangaea, and the environment was perfect for the cold-blooded reptiles. Different species of reptiles in different places reproduced in great numbers, and like other forms of life before them found themselves competing with each other for food in an overcrowded environment. Only those who were good at fighting or running away survived. Some species of dinosaurs had gigantic bodies that helped them compete for food, and the ground shook under the footfalls of creatures like brontosaurus, stegosaurus, and tyrannosaurus.

Dinosaurs and other reptiles (including the flying pterodactyls) spread to all the environments of the Earth. They were the dominant animals for about 125 million years.

But even in the years that the Earth had a warm climate, it was cool at night. The most fearsome reptiles slowed down and became sluggish after dark as their bodies cooled down. Because their body temperature kept going up and down between day and night, reptiles didn't have large or complicated brains. These can only evolve when the body temperature remains constant.

But having small, simple brains didn't keep reptiles from surviving. Their DNA carried instincts that told them all they needed to know: EAT, REPRODUCE, RUN AWAY FROM DANGER, FIGHT AND KILL IF NECESSARY—SURVIVE. Even with very little intelligence, reptiles were the top animals on Earth for about 125 million years.

Birds and Mammals

As reptiles dominated the Earth, two new kinds of animals evolved from branches of the reptile family: birds and **mammals.** Birds survived because they could take to the air and escape land predators. Mammals survived because they could remain active at night, when reptiles were cooled down and sluggish. This was possible because mammals (and birds as well) were **warm-blooded**—they could keep their bodies warm even when it was cold outside. Warm-blooded animals had chemical reactions inside their bodies that produced heat from the food they ate. They also had feathers or fur that kept the heat in and insulated them from cold weather.

Some mammals ate only plants. But others discovered that the most delicious meals around were to be found by breaking open reptiles' eggs and eating their nutritious contents. After dark, most reptiles were too slowed down to catch mammals. Over the years the new night hunters gobbled up countless eggs, keeping many reptiles from being born.

But during the daytime it was a different story. Mammals

spent most of their time hiding or running away from the bigger, stronger reptiles. One theory as to how the mammals kept from being eaten by reptiles is that they slept during the daylight hours. If mammals were quietly slumbering in their nests, they were less likely to be found and more likely to survive. Those mammals with an instinct to sleep during the day survived and passed on that behavior to their young.

Because mammals are warm-blooded, their body temperatures stayed fairly constant, and this meant that some species of mammals evolved with much better brains than reptiles. But even though the mammals were smarter and could sneak around at night stealing the reptiles' eggs, their cold-blooded cousins still got most of the food, and only small and nimble mammals survived long enough to reproduce.

The Great Extinction

Then about 65 million years ago, all the dinosaurs suddenly died out. So did many other creatures on land and in the sea. Only small reptiles like snakes, lizards, and crocodiles survived. What could have caused so many species of living things to become extinct so suddenly? Scientists aren't sure, and this remains one of the great mysteries of the story of life.

The most believable theory is that the Earth's climate got cooler, which changed the environments to which many animals were adapted. In the case of the dinosaurs, they became too sluggish to hunt for food during the daytime, and gradually starved to death. Their bodies could not adapt to the sudden

The dinosaurs became extinct about 65 million years ago. One theory is that the world's temperature dropped, and these creatures were not able to survive the cold. Unfortunately for them, they didn't have big-enough brains or clever-enough hands to knit sweaters or build fires.

change in climate, and their brains weren't clever enough for them to make clothes or build fires to keep warm.

There is a new theory that, unlike other reptiles, dinosaurs were warm-blooded, and a lively debate is going on among the dinosaur experts. If dinosaurs were warm-blooded, perhaps it was not the cooler climate that killed them off, but something else. One theory is that there was a supernova near the Earth, and the radiation from the exploding star killed the largest animals, among them the dinosaurs. Another theory is that a new kind of plant food gave the dinosaurs indigestion and led to their sudden extinction.

Whatever the reason, the dinosaurs disappeared from the Earth, and life became a lot easier for the mammals. They could now begin to move around during the daytime and take their pick from a large variety of food. Mammals with larger bodies not only survived, but became the dominant animals on Earth.

6

Mammals and Primates

Mammals were different from their reptile cousins in six important ways. First, they were warm-blooded, so their body temperature stayed about the same despite changes in the weather. Second, mammals had more complex brains, made possible by their more consistent body temperature. Third, they had better eyesight than most reptiles. This was because for millions of years, warm-blooded mammals had looked for their food after dark, and only those with excellent eyesight had survived.

A fourth difference was in the way mammals ate. Reptiles swallowed their food whole, then sat around for hours while their stomachs digested it. But most mammals had flat chewing teeth called **molars** with which they could grind up their food before they swallowed it. This made their stomach's job easier, and gave them a faster and more constant supply of energy from their food.

A fifth difference between mammals and reptiles was the way in which they gave birth to their young. Reptile mothers laid their offspring in tough-shelled eggs, and left them to develop, hatch, and grow up on their own. When young reptiles broke out of their shells, they had to be ready to make it by themselves, because usually their parents were not around.

Birds, which branched off from the reptile family and evolved to be warm-blooded, kept the reptile system of giving birth to their young in hard-shelled eggs. But unlike the reptiles, birds had to sit on their eggs to keep their developing offspring from getting cold. What's more, when most young birds hatched, they were helpless and dependent on their parents to bring them food until they could survive on their own.

Mammals had evolved a step further. Their young grew inside the mother's body in an area called the **uterus**. This new system kept developing mammals warm and safe while their mothers looked for food and ran away from danger. Mammals didn't grow a hard shell around them inside the uterus, and they were born naked to the world and completely dependent on their mothers.

The sixth difference between mammals and reptiles was that mammal mothers were able to produce milk through nipples on the undersides of their bodies. This milk nourished their young until they were strong enough to find their own food. If newborn mammals didn't get milk, warmth, and protection from their mothers, they died. So it was important to the survival of mammals that mothers have a set of instincts which told them to take care of their young. This was the beginning of motherly love.

New Continents

During these years of mammal evolution, the supercontinent Pangaea was breaking up into several smaller continents. Forces inside the Earth moved many tons of rock and dirt and plants and animals inch by inch, and gradually the new continents moved apart like giant rafts. New bodies of water formed between them, and grew an inch or two wider every year until they were oceans more than a thousand miles wide. Animals and plants that had once lived side by side were now completely cut off from one another.

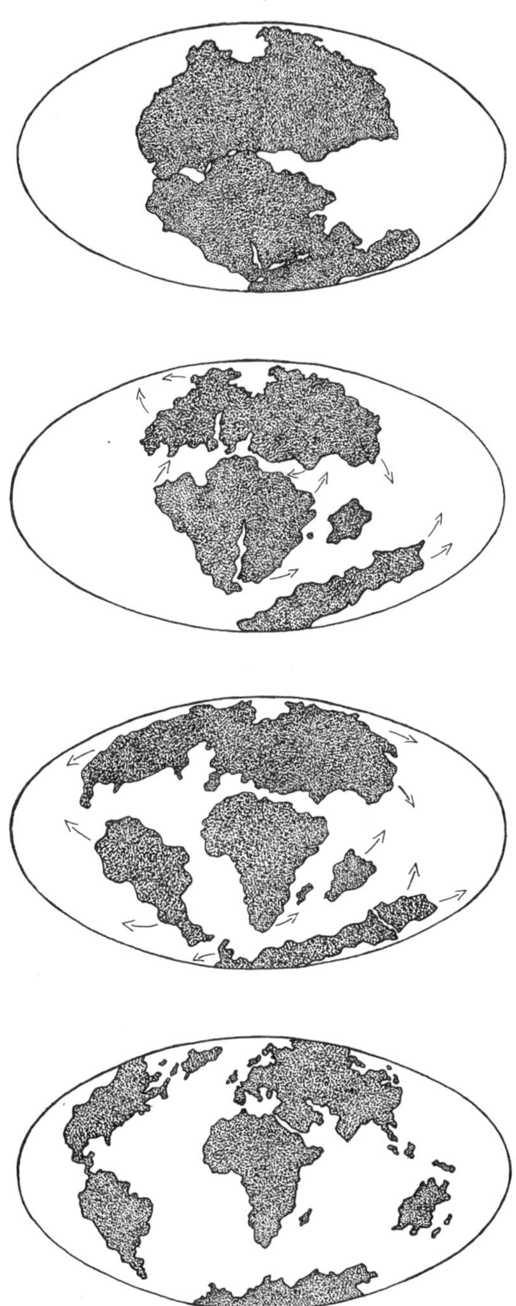

Over millions of years, Pangaea (which included all the dry land on Earth) broke up into several smaller continents. The continents are still moving (very slowly) from each other today.

Each of the new land masses (which became Asia, India, Europe, Africa, Australia, Antarctica, North America, and South America) had different environments, and only animals and plants that were well adapted could survive. Life branched in many different directions according to the environment, and the Earth was populated with animals as diverse as elephants and bears, mice and rabbits, kangaroos and tigers, llamas and giraffes—not to mention all the reptiles, plants, insects, and other forms of life on land and sea.

New species did fine as long as their environment stayed the same and as long as they didn't leave that environment. Species could even adapt if the environments changed slowly, because there were usually enough variations and mutations in the DNA for a few to survive in slightly different conditions.

But if the environment changed too quickly (as probably happened in the case of the dinosaurs), a species was done for. The polar bear was adapted to living in a cold, snow-covered environment, and died if the climate became hotter and the snow melted. The camel had evolved to survive in the desert with very little water, and didn't do well if the desert turned into a swamp. The giraffe had evolved to survive in open grassland without many trees, and could not make it in a thick jungle. If animals were taken out of the environments to which they were adapted, they were like fish out of water. Animals were trapped; they were prisoners of their own evolution.

Primates

Not all mammals had large bodies like bears and tigers and elephants; some species were quick, mouselike creatures similar to the species that lived in the days of the dinosaurs. As these creatures scurried around looking for food, they had to avoid being eaten by larger meat-eating mammals. One good way of escaping danger was to climb trees.

An imaginary scene showing some of the different species of mammals (and one bird) that evolved after the giant reptiles became extinct 65 million years ago.

Originally, no mammal's body was very well suited to holding on to tree trunks and balancing on branches. In fact, trees were a very difficult environment that required a whole new set of adaptations. Twigs and branches could break at any moment. Leaves moving in the sunlight and shadows could be confusing. A gust of wind could easily throw a small animal off balance. Mammals that took refuge in the trees were in constant danger of falling.

Probably most of the small mammals that climbed trees fell into the jaws of their pursuers. But a few—maybe only one in a thousand—happened to have paws that could grip a little better, and they didn't fall. Being able to escape into the trees gave these few such an advantage over ground-dwelling mammals that they multiplied and passed their fortunate adaptations along to their young. Before long, there were many kinds of small mammals living in the trees, and they competed with each other for food.

Over millions of years of natural selection, the only tree dwellers that survived were those with very quick reactions, good judgment, excellent balance and coordination, and feet that could grip the trunks and branches of trees. All the poorly adapted tree-dwelling mammals died out, and a new kind of animal emerged—the **primates**. Their bodies were totally adapted to life in the trees.

Primates reproduced, outgrew their food supply, and slowly evolved and spread to many of the jungles and forests around the world. Among the species adapted to different environments were **lemurs** (which were probably closest to the original primates), monkeys, orangutans, chimpanzees, baboons, and gorillas. The primates that lived in a thick jungle environment spent all their time in the trees and had tails that could grip the branches. Others that lived in forests with more clearings spent part of their time on the ground and had larger bodies without tails.

When they first evolved about 75 million years ago, these creatures were the most highly developed, intelligent form of life on Earth. They had paws with soft pads and separate fingers for gripping branches, and thumbs that could wrap around the opposite side of a branch from the other four fingers for a better grip (called an **opposable thumb**). They had enough coordination to pick up small seeds and insects and put them in their mouths, which most mammals with paws couldn't do.

Primates had **stereoscopic eyes**, which means that both eyeballs pointed forward and could accurately gauge the distance between branches. This set them apart from other animals (lizards and fish, for example) whose eyes were on either side of their heads. Primates also had brains with the very complicated "wiring" (inner connections) needed to coordinate a body moving quickly through the trees. Their brains could calculate distances, sense whether branches would hold their weight, take wind speed into account, remember the complex structure of trees, and make split-second decisions about which way to jump in an emergency.

Because they were constantly moving through the trees to get food and escape danger, primates couldn't take care of more than one or two offspring at a time. Over the years, the trait of having small litters became part of primates' DNA. The fast-moving life of the treetops also meant that they couldn't stop in one place and take care of helpless newborn primates. By natural selection, the survivors were those who happened to give birth to offspring that could move around and cling to their mothers as soon as they were born, and this trait was passed along.

Almost all primates were (and still are) **social animals**, which means that they spend most of their time in groups. Sticking together was important for finding food (mainly plant life) and warning each other of danger. To cooperate with other members of their groups, primates had to have strong and complex

This is what one of the early primates might have looked like. With its stereoscopic eyes and specialized feet, it was well adapted for life in the treetops.

emotions—instinctive feelings of love, loyalty, jealousy, hate, and so on. Without these emotions, primates would not have been able to work together and survive. A whole section of their brain had evolved to process these complicated thoughts, a section that didn't exist in the brains of reptiles, fish, and invertebrates.

Modern chimpanzees aren't very different from their ancestors of millions of years ago, and scientists have been able to study them closely to get clues about how primates evolved. One primate expert named Jane Goodall has spent years observing the behavior of chimpanzees in Africa. She has found that they are highly intelligent creatures who are capable of intense loyalty and love and jealousy. She has also found that they can resort to brutality and murder among their own kind under certain circumstances.

The Trees Thin Out

About 45 million years ago, the gradual movement of land masses once again changed environments in many parts of the world. Several of the huge land "rafts" collided, crunching together and inch by inch pushing up mountain ranges several miles into the sky. These mountains (the Rockies, Andes, and Himalayas) blocked and changed the flow of wind currents around the world, which led to a slight drop in the temperature and a decrease in rainfall.

The drier conditions caused some of the dense jungles that covered large parts of Africa and Asia to thin out, opening up grasslands with few trees. Primates retreated to the remaining jungles. But in the eastern part of Africa, the primates were trapped. At that time, a chain of lakes in the Great Rift Valley separated this area from the rest of Africa. The trees in East Africa thinned out and the jungles were replaced by grasslands, and primates that had lived in the trees were cut off from the remaining jungles of Africa. The lakes trapped them in an environment that was rapidly changing. They had no choice but to spend more and more time on the ground.

Could they survive outside the treetop environment to which their bodies were adapted? Not the small primates. They were quickly gobbled up by predators on the ground. But some of the larger primates did survive, and they did so because of the very adaptations that had originally helped their ancestors

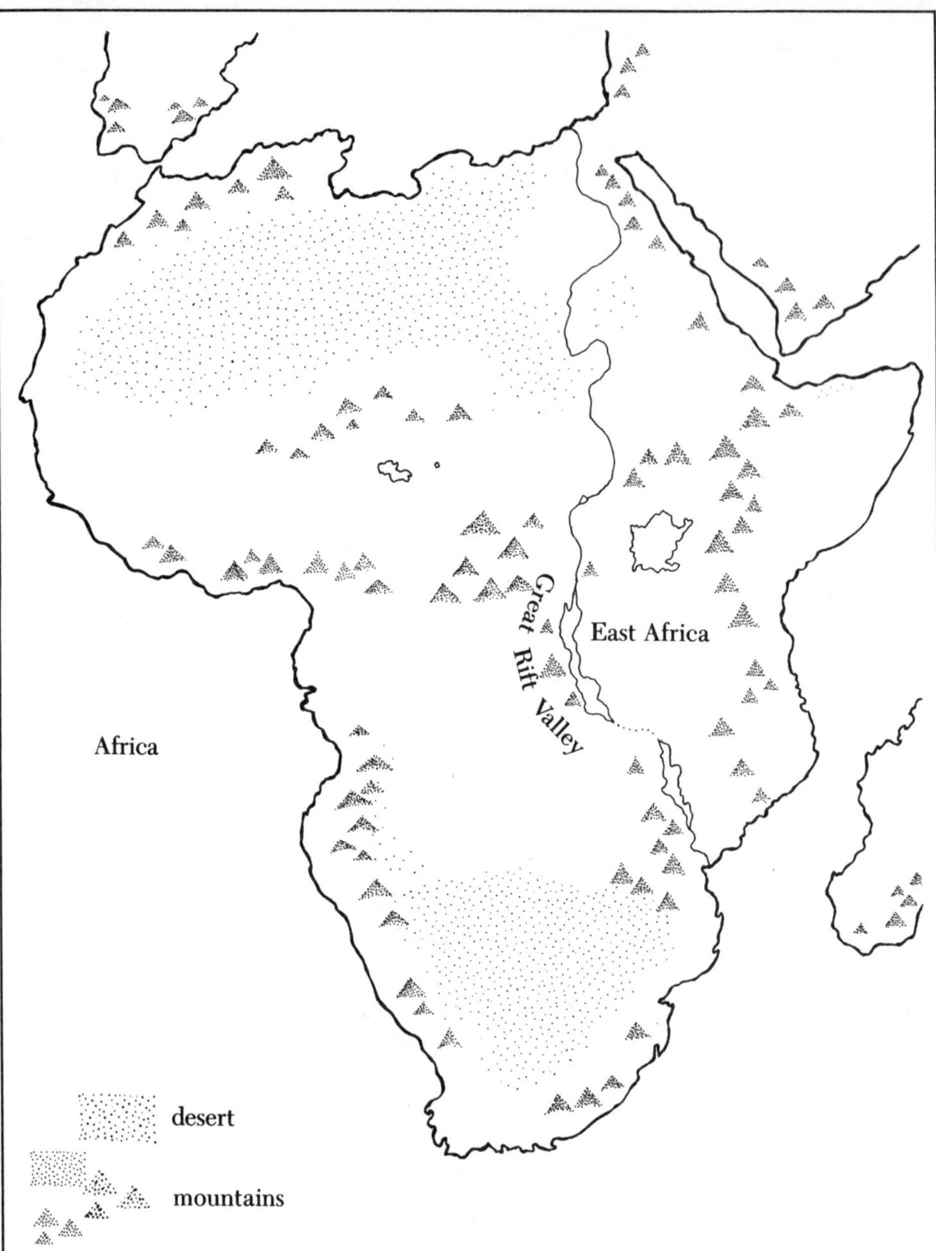

The lakes in the Great Rift Valley of Africa cut off the primates of East Africa from the jungles in other parts of the continent. As the jungles died out, these primates were forced to spend more and more of their time on the ground.

survive in the trees—skillful hands, stereoscopic eyes, a highly developed brain, and the ability to stick together in groups.

As these primates came down from the dying trees in East Africa (and possibly in other parts of Africa and Asia), the evolution of life on Earth was about to take a giant step. Most scientists think these ground-dwelling primates were the direct ancestors of human beings.

7

The Hominids

The idea that humans are descended from animals surprises most people when they first hear it. We think of ourselves as being much smarter than animals, and it's hard to picture how our bodies could have evolved from primates, mammals, reptiles, amphibians, fish, and cells. To many people, it seems more logical that humans were created out of thin air by an all-powerful god.

That's what most people believed until about a hundred years ago. Then a scientist named Charles Darwin wrote two books in which he put forward the idea that all living things evolved by natural selection, gradually changing to fit into different environments. When Darwin's books came out, they caused a sensation around the world. Many people were shocked by the idea that humans were related to all animals and plants. They thought people were above nature, not a part of it. There were many heated arguments about Darwin's theory of evolution. Many people hated Darwin for it, and some of them insulted him in cruel ways. In some places Darwinian theory is still not taught, or is offered as a possible alternative theory to a creation by a god.

But in the years since Darwin's books were published, thousands of scientists have tested his theories and come to agree with him. There are three kinds of evidence that seem to connect humans to the world of animals and plants.

First, scientists have found many fossils of creatures in between primates and humans. They call these **hominids**, which means "of the family of humans." The bones of hominids strongly suggest that gradually, over millions of years, one branch of primates evolved into human beings.

Second, there are many clues inside the human body which suggest that we have evolved from other forms of life. For instance, the appendix is now a useless part of our intestine, but years ago it had a function in a slightly different digestive system. Another example is the muscles attached to our ears. Most people can't control them (do you know any people who can wiggle their ears?), but scientists think that many years ago, muscles like these were very important to our ancestors' survival. Being able to move their ears around helped animals hear the slightest sound of approaching danger.

We also have fluids inside our bodies that are salty (think of tears and sweat; even our blood is salty). Scientists think this goes back to the time when our ancestors the fish lived in the salty oceans, evolved with fluids inside their bodies like the water around them, and passed that trait along.

Another clue is the different stages we go through as we develop inside our mother's uterus. Before being born, all humans at one point have gills, as fish embryos do. A little later we have tails, like embryos of other mammals inside their mothers. We grow out of these stages before we are born. But these are more pieces of evidence that our way-back ancestors were indeed animals.

A third kind of evidence lies in the chemicals inside the human body. Modern scientists have analyzed these chemicals and found that they are exactly the same as those in animals and plants. All life on Earth is basically made of amino acids and nucleotide bases, with the supermolecule DNA carrying the instructions for creating future generations. The only differences between flowers, trees, fish, lizards, tigers, elephants, and humans lie in the way the chemicals are arranged and the message that is carried by the DNA. This suggests that we are all branches of the same tree of life.

Ramapithecus and the Hominids

Scientists have found a few fossils of the first ground-dwelling primates and given them a Latin name—***Ramapithecus***. No complete skeletons have been found, and it's not clear whether members of *Ramapithecus* were hominids or their immediate ancestors.

In any case, these creatures lived about 14 million years ago in an environment filled with animals on the prowl for food—lions, hyenas, wild dogs, and many others. *Ramapithecus* didn't have large claws, fighting teeth, poisonous fangs, sharp beaks, or any other special equipment built into its body. It wasn't even a very fast runner compared to some predators. *Ramapithecus* could still climb trees. But what if it got caught in the open with no trees around? How could it keep from being wiped out by the more highly adapted ground animals? How could it make up for its lack of special equipment?

Many were killed. But those who survived were the ones that stuck together in groups and took advantage of their skillful hands, good eyesight, and superior brains. When they were threatened by predators, they probably picked up sticks (their tree-adapted hands were perfect for that), reared up on their hind legs (that made them seem bigger), bared their teeth, made lots of noise, and threw rocks. In the world of animals, bluffing is often more important than fighting. If they banded together and tricked other animals into thinking they were gangs of fierce monsters, they often didn't have to fight and were able to avoid being eaten. Any who strayed from the

This imaginary scene shows a *Ramapithecus* on the edge of open grasslands. Although its body was not specially adapted to life in the grasslands, *Ramapithecus* had a clever-enough brain and skillful-enough hands to survive.

group and didn't learn how to use these tricks were quickly killed by predators.

Because it was living in a completely different environment, *Ramapithecus* evolved further and further away from its ancestors in the treetops. Those with small advantages (a better brain, more skillful hands, a larger body) had a better chance of survival, and gradually *Ramapithecus* evolved into new species of hominids that looked more and more like modern humans.

One of the most important evolutionary changes that took place was walking upright on two feet. Those hominids who happened to stand upright had several advantages. They could see over the top of tall grass and get an earlier warning of predators creeping up on them. They could scare away predators because they appeared to be bigger than hominids that walked on all fours. Upright walking also left two hands free to carry food and sticks. All this meant that the hominids who walked on their hind legs survived and superseded those who didn't. Standing up straight involved big changes in hominids' feet, pelvises, and the way the backbones were attached to the heads (which sat on top instead of hanging forward), so the change must have taken millions of years of gradual DNA changes.

What did early hominids eat? To answer this question, scientists have looked at the teeth of the fossils they've found, and have concluded that the diet of these creatures probably consisted of insects, seeds, fruits, and other forms of plant life. At this point it included almost no meat. Scientists can tell this in two ways.

First, the hominids' teeth were not shaped in a way that would have been effective for tearing apart raw meat. And second, there are tiny scratches on the fossilized teeth which came from the grains of sand and dirt in the plant life these hominids were chewing. From this evidence, it seems that the first hominids weren't hunters, and that they only occasionally ate meat. They probably used sticks to scare away other animals, poke around for tasty roots, and break open bones to eat the marrow—but not to kill other animals.

Homo habilis

The best-adapted hominids survived, reproduced, and spread gradually to many parts of Africa and Asia. There has been a dramatic increase in the number of hominid fossils dug up in the last few years. One family of scientists—Mary and Louis Leakey and their son Richard Leakey—has been particularly successful in finding fossils in East Africa. Slowly scientists are piecing together a picture of what hominids looked like between 2 and 3 million years ago.

The fossils show that there were at least three species of hominid living in Africa at that time. Scientists have given the ones they have discovered Latin names: There were ***Australopithecus africanus***, a slim hominid that grew to be about four feet tall; ***Australopithecus robustus***, a more heavyset hominid that grew to about five feet tall; and ***Homo habilis***, which had the largest and most complicated brain of all the hominids so far.

All three of these hominid species are extinct, as are other species of hominids that lived millions of years ago. But one species—*Homo habilis*—was probably the branch of the hominid family that led to modern humans. Most scientists think that the two *Australopithecus* branches were dead ends, while *Homo habilis* continued to evolve into more intelligent hominids.

Why did the members of *Homo habilis* survive to pass on their DNA to future generations while the others did not? One theory is that they had four characteristics which gave them a competitive advantage over other hominids.

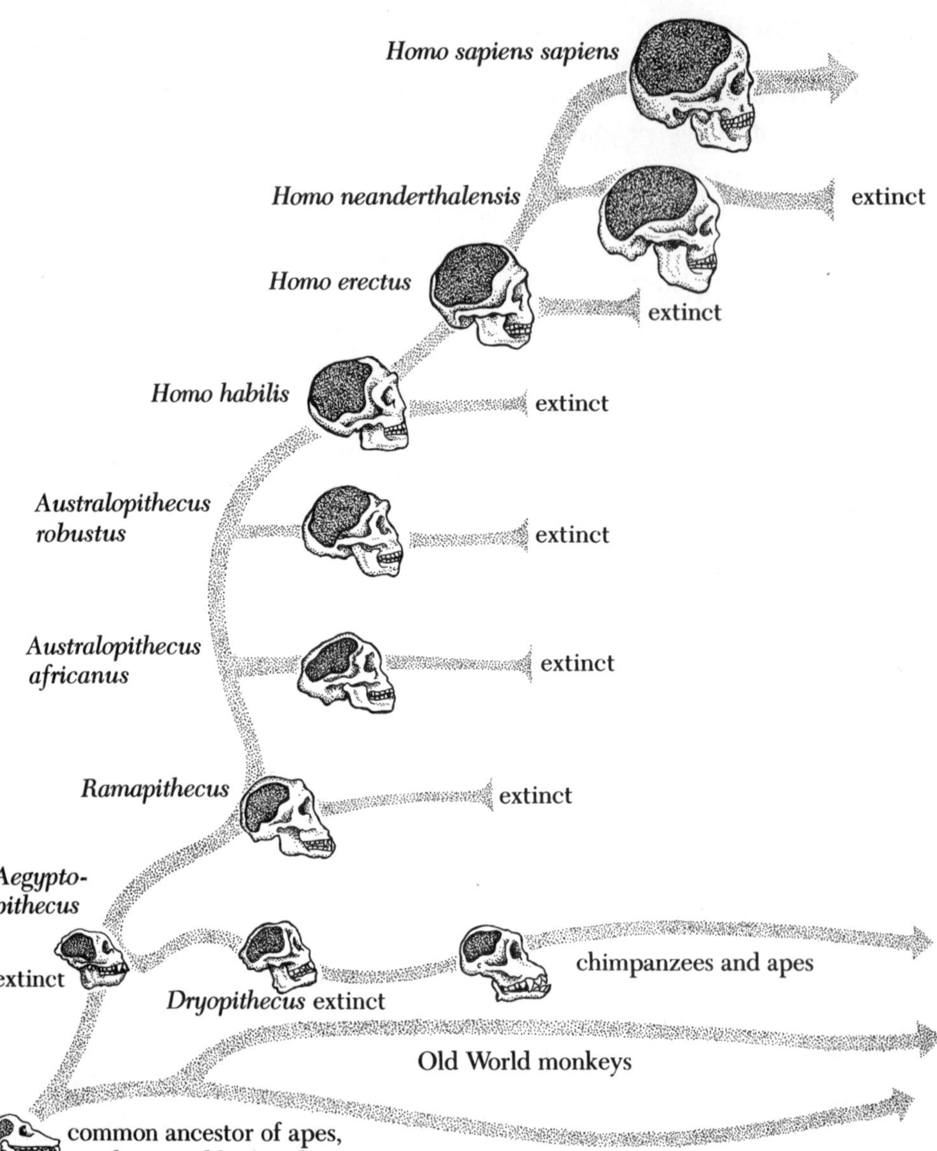

Starting at the bottom, these drawings show one theory of the evolution of modern humans from an early mammal ancestor. The shaded area inside each skull is the brain, which gradually evolved to be bigger and more complex over the years.

First, *Homo habilis* had begun to eat meat. The evidence from the teeth of ancient hominids is that only *Homo habilis* was a regular meat eater, while other hominids stuck mainly to plants and insects. It probably began when some *Homo habilis* found a half-eaten animal carcass, scared away the predators that had killed it, and helped themselves. Eating meat gave those who tried it a real advantage, because an **omnivorous** diet (one consisting of plants and meat) supplied them with more protein and made their bodies bigger, stronger, and more energetic than one consisting of just plants alone.

Hominids who had a taste for meat survived, passed that trait on in their DNA, and taught their offspring how to find meat. Over the years meat eaters became more effective scavengers, and eventually they began to do their own hunting. The first hominid hunters probably copied the techniques of the wild dogs and hyenas they competed with, stalking their prey from downwind and picking out the weakest animals in a herd to make the kill easier. Catching fast-moving animals wasn't easy, and hominids only succeeded if they worked as teams and used every bit of intelligence and planning ability in their brains.

A second characteristic that helped *Homo habilis* survive was that they had learned how to use stones as weapons and tools. Stones were harder, heavier, and sharper than the sticks and bones used by other hominids, and those who used them had a considerable advantage. Stone users passed the idea down to future generations, and as time went by hominids became more careful about the stones they used. They picked up only those that were sharp and easy to hold in the palms of their hands, and instead of dropping their stones when they got through using them, they began to carry their favorite tools and weapons around for future use.

Third, *Homo habilis* had a somewhat larger and more complicated brain. During the years that the abilities to walk up-

The hands that had originally evolved to hold on to branches were very adaptable to picking up branches as weapons, and later picking up rocks and using them as weapons and tools. Over millions of years of evolution, hominid hands became more and more skillful, until they could perform very precise tasks.

right, eat meat, and use stones were evolving, the brain size of these hominids gradually increased, and the "wiring" inside became more and more intricate. Scientists have pieced together the skulls of some hominids and measured the amount of space inside where the brain used to be. They know that by about 3 million years ago, *Homo habilis* had the largest and most complex brain of all hominids—in fact possibly the most complex of any animal on Earth. The improved brain could control increasingly skillful hands, help to outsmart animals, and plan for the future.

What's more, these larger brains seem to have contained an area that helped *Homo habilis* work and get along with other members of the group in a closer way than was true for more primitive primates and other hominids. Some scientists think this took more brainpower than anything else, and was vitally important to the survival of this kind of hominid.

Fourth, *Homo habilis* seems to have lived in camps and

brought the food from hunting and gathering back to share with the whole group. Some scientists think this was the most important difference between *Homo habilis* and the other hominids, who ate their food right where they found it, were constantly on the move, and didn't set up camps.

Scientists have dug up the remains of *Homo habilis* camps in East Africa, complete with animal bones, hominid remains, and stone tools and weapons. It appears that these hominids stayed in one place for several weeks at a time, scouting in all directions to find plant food and meat to carry back to the camp. As they shared their food, they must also have shared ideas on where to get food the next day, which predators to look out for, which plants were poisonous, and so on.

So while *Homo habilis* became an accomplished stone-using hunter and gatherer and shared food and experiences within the groups, the other hominids continued a hand-to-mouth existence and didn't develop hunting or stone tools and weapons to any great extent. Over the next million years, the two *Australopithecus* species were caught between more successful *Homo habilis* and various animals competing for the same food. While the descendants of *Homo habilis* survived and continued to evolve, the other hominids died out.

In the years that followed, the most successful hominids evolved with more skillful hands, taller bodies, and better brains, all of which allowed them to make better tools and weapons, become better hunters, and work more effectively with their fellow hominids. This continuing evolution took place for the usual reasons—those with small advantages survived and passed them along in their DNA. But there was another reason for the rapid evolution of hominids: The characteristics listed above were **mutually reinforcing**, which means they helped each other along.

Standing upright helped hominids use stones because it freed their hands, which let more skillful hands evolve, which led to improvements in the brain to control them—which made it even more important that they stand upright all the time. Eating meat encouraged hominids to find better stones and use them more cleverly, and hunting meat required close cooperation between hominids, all of which pushed along the evolution of the brain and skillful hands—which helped them catch more meat.

The evolution of more complex brains helped hominids think ahead, save their tools and weapons, cooperate better with other hominids, and get more food—all of which led to the evolution of brains that were more complex and intelligent. Carrying food to the camp and sharing it with the group helped along the evolution of intelligence and gave *Homo habilis* more chance to share ideas and pass them along to future generations.

Thus the evolution of more and more intelligent and skillful and cooperative hominids continued over the years.

8

Homo erectus

Scientists think *Homo habilis* lived in groups of twenty-five to thirty, and divided up the jobs between male and female members of the group. The males did the hunting, while females gathered plant food and did most of the child rearing. This division of labor probably evolved because of the time and energy the females had to devote to bearing, giving birth to, and nursing their young so that the species could survive.

Hunting was exciting and dangerous, but hunters often had bad days and came back to camp empty-handed. Hominid groups would not have survived without the plant food gathered by females, which supplied more than two thirds of the food eaten by these groups. The most important inventions used by females for gathering food were probably sharpened sticks to dig up roots and carrier bags to collect nuts, berries, and other small fruits.

The reason you don't hear too much about carrier bags and sharpened sticks in books about hominids is that these food-gathering implements rotted away over the years, leaving no traces. It's only guesswork that leads scientists to think this is how hominids gathered the plant life that kept them alive. But the stone weapons used by the hunters were a different story.

They lasted well over the millions of years since they were used, and scientists know a great deal about how hominids chipped stones to do different jobs—killing, scraping, cutting, etc. The cleverest hominids discovered that one kind of stone, **flint**, was easy to sharpen and made effective tools and weapons. Scientists have found many of these crude stone implements among the animal and hominid bones of 2–3 million years ago.

Male and female hominids did very important jobs for their groups, and couldn't live without each other's contributions. Because they needed each other so much, males and females were pulled together in close family relationships. Unlike most other animals, these hominids were probably **monogamous**, which means each male and female chose one mate, had children, and stayed together with the same mate for a long period of time. Hominid children had relatively long childhoods, during which they were dependent on their parents and the group. This made it even more important for the family and the group to stick together and share the work.

All the sharing of food and information in these camps led to the development of language, which was the quickest and easiest way of communicating ideas. Scientists think that by 2 million years ago, *Homo habilis* was using words and sentences to get ideas across. The first words were spoken long before that, probably imitations of the sounds made by animals (a growl for a tiger, a hiss for a snake) accompanied by hand gestures. Over the years, hominids gradually made up words for the things they saw around them and the feelings of love, jealousy, fear, and so on which they wanted to express.

Those who happened to have better mouths and vocal cords could make a greater variety of sounds and communicate better, so they survived and passed on to their children the ability to speak more clearly. They also passed down the words they had invented—but these had to be learned by children, since DNA can't hold words, only the capacity to use them. Those hominids who didn't use language were less likely to be able to work together as hunters, escape danger, find food, or plan for the future, so they gradually died out.

Outward Migration

There was a good reason why the ideal group size for hominids was between twenty-five and thirty. With this number of *Homo habilis* in one camp, there were about eight adult males to go out hunting and enough females to do the gathering, and there weren't too many mouths to feed. Each group gathered and hunted in the area around its camp and moved when the food supply was used up—probably five or six times a year. Each of these small bands of hominids probably had ties to a larger tribe of about 500 spread over a wider area. The 16–20 groups in a tribe stayed in touch, constantly sharing ideas about tools and weapons and exchanging members through intermarriage.

Homo habilis reproduced and increased in number, and in some places the small groups began to get in each other's way. If too many hunted and gathered in too small an area, there wasn't enough food for everyone; each group needed its own elbow room. There may have been some fights between groups of hominids over territory. But a more common reaction to an overcrowded hunting ground was for one group to move a mile or so away. If a group grew much larger than thirty, some of its members formed a new group and moved away to find its own area in which to do its hunting and gathering.

Slowly, a mile or two at a time, hominids spread out over a wider and wider area of Africa. By 1½ million years ago, some had moved into Asia by crossing the narrow land bridge in what is now Egypt. In the thousands of years that followed, hominids spread to the eastern end of Asia and north into Europe. Many hominid fossils have been found in various places around these continents. The hominids of this era had brains and bodies that were quite a bit bigger and more refined than those of their ancestors. Scientists have another Latin name for the new species—***Homo erectus***.

By moving thousands of miles from their origins and surviving in many different environments, hominids were doing something that no other animal could do. As we have shown, animals and other forms of life couldn't survive outside the environments to which their bodies were adapted. When there were too many in one area, some died of starvation and the best adapted survived. But hominids were different. They could carry tools and food and water with them, and were clever enough to survive in almost any environment. When there were too many hominids in one place, some simply moved on to another place. In this way, *Homo erectus* gradually spread around the world, and the population of intelligent, adaptable hominids steadily increased, limited only by the food supply of the planet Earth.

Fire

As hominids moved away from the warm regions around the equator, they encountered chillier nights and colder winters. There was less plant life to gather, and hunting became more important to survival. Hominids invented better weapons like spears, axes, and harpoons, formed bigger hunting groups, and went after larger animals. They also began to take refuge in caves or build primitive shelters for themselves out of branches and mud. But their most important discovery in this era was fire.

Hominids had seen bolts of lightning start forest and brush fires. Like other creatures, they were terrified of the hot, roaring flames. But at some point (no one is sure when) hominids got up the courage to pick up a burning stick and bring it back to camp to start their own controlled fires. A campfire was a great help to survival, since it scared away predators and gave the hominids in the group warmth at night and in the winter. When hominids moved into caves, they usually had to kick out bears or other wild animals. Lighting a fire in the entrance of the cave kept the former tenants from getting any ideas about moving back in.

The problem was that hominids were dependent on a bolt of lightning to start each fire. If the fire went out, they might have to wait for weeks for another thunderstorm. But then some clever hominids discovered that they could start their own fires by striking flint stones together and catching the sparks that flew off in some dried grass, or by rubbing sticks until they began to smolder. Hominids in different places may have come up with these brilliant inventions independently; wherever they were made, they must have spread quickly from camp to camp and tribe to tribe.

The ability to light a fire at any time the group wanted one made it easier for hominids to survive in colder areas of the world. It extended even more the number of different environments in which these remarkable creatures could live. Campfires also pulled hominid groups together after dark and further encouraged the development of language and culture. As hominids sat around their fires in a circle, they stared into the flickering flames and talked about what had happened that day and what they planned for tomorrow.

Hominids may also have begun to tell stories about their exploits and create myths and rituals to deal with their fears about animals, lightning, thunder, tornadoes, volcanoes, earthquakes, and other powerful natural forces they didn't understand.

The idea of cooking food probably occurred to hominids

when someone accidentally dropped a piece of raw meat into a fire, pulled it out, and noticed that it tasted better and was easier to chew when it was cooked. The idea spread rapidly, and influenced the evolution of hominids' faces over the years. As hominids ate cooked meat and chewing became less difficult, they didn't need such massive jawbones and muscles. Over the next few thousand generations, those who happened to be born with more refined faces (which were better adapted to talking than chewing raw meat) survived, passed down these DNA instructions, and gradually replaced the large-jawed hominids.

Brutal Savages?

How did the lives of these hominids a million years ago compare with ours today? Was life short and nasty and brutal as they struggled to survive in competition with other hominids and countless predators? Some people think not. Based on their observations of modern hunter-gatherers in Africa, some scientists think our ancestors one million years ago had developed an excellent way of getting and sharing food. According to this theory, ancient hunter-gatherers had to work only about twenty hours a week, compared to the forty-hour work week of most humans in our country today. To be sure, life was a day-to-day proposition, and hominids were afflicted by disease and disaster and constant uncertainty. But these ancient hominids may have had a more leisurely life-style than many creatures before or since.

Some scientists argue that when hominids became hunters, they were fierce and aggressive creatures who killed their own kind as well as the animals they hunted. According to this theory, there were frequent wars between tribes of hominids, they were often cannibals, and their DNA carried messages that made them (and their descendants, human beings) naturally aggressive.

An imaginary scene showing some members of a hominid group at their campsite.

But other scientists don't agree. They think that the most important messages in the DNA and brains of these hominids were those that made them share food and ideas and work cooperatively in groups. These scientists agree that hominids were capable of aggression and violence under certain conditions, but think they were too spread out and too occupied with the day-to-day business of getting food at this point to fight wars. Besides, they had no way of gathering enough food in a small area of land to supply an army.

According to this theory, the lives of early hominids were mostly peaceful, and wars only began later, in the days of "civilized" humans.

9

Homo sapiens sapiens

As *Homo erectus* reproduced and spread around Africa, Asia, and Europe, it competed with animals and other hominids for survival, and only those with the most effective bodies, brains, and patterns of behavior made it. By 500,000 years ago, some hominids had taller and more powerful bodies, larger brains, a more dome-shaped skull, smaller teeth, and smaller bony ridges over their eyes. Scientists have found fossils of this new species in many parts of the world, and have named it ***Homo sapiens***. These hominids had bodies almost the same as modern humans, and they gradually spread out and replaced the earlier hominids.

The part of the hominid brain that was gradually getting larger is known as the **neocortex**. It is unlike anything that other animals have inside their heads, and its intricate "wiring" gave hominids the ability to use language, plan for the future, solve problems, and get along with other hominids in the group. Those with a better-developed neocortex survived, and those with smaller, less complex brains didn't.

But there was one problem with the bigger brains and skulls with which hominids were being born: It was difficult for a bigger-brained baby to fit through its mother's **birth canal**. Larger brains may have been an advantage for surviving in the world, but they were no good if babies' heads were so big that both mother and child died in childbirth.

Some scientists speculate that over thousands of generations, this problem was solved in two ways. First, females evolved with wider pelvises, so there was more room for babies with larger heads to be born. This change happened in the usual way that new traits evolve: Females with narrow pelvises died in childbirth or gave birth to smaller-brained babies, who had less chance of survival when they grew up.

But those females who happened to have wider pelvises didn't die in childbirth. They gave birth to larger-brained babies, and passed along the trait of the wider pelvis to their daughters and a larger brain to all their children. These children had better chances of surviving in the world. Over the years, hominids who had those two traits in their DNA replaced those who didn't. Brains continued to grow larger, and females' pelvises gradually widened.

But there is a limit to how wide a pelvis can become before it begins to interfere with walking and running. Female hominids still had to be able to move quickly to escape danger and do their part for the survival of the group. Females who had super-wide pelvises were awkward and ungainly, and they didn't live very long. Only females with medium-wide pelvises could survive—and this put a limit on the brain size of their babies.

But there was a second evolutionary change that got around this limit. Some babies were born before the full term of pregnancy, when their skulls hadn't yet grown to full size. A baby born before its full term was smaller and had less trouble passing through its mother's birth canal. Now both the mother and baby could survive childbirth, and the baby could finish its development and growth outside the mother's body. Mothers who happened to have the DNA trait for giving birth before the full term of pregnancy could have larger-brained babies without dying in childbirth or having an ungainly pelvis. So a package of three DNA messages was passed along to future generations: a larger brain, a medium-width pelvis, and the trait of giving birth to babies before full term. This made possible a continued enlargement of the brain size of *Homo sapiens*.

Naturally the hominids who had these three traits survived, and they gradually replaced those who didn't. Eventually the length of pregnancy settled at around nine months, which is what it is among humans today. Without this shortened pregnancy, the full term would be eighteen months—but of course no baby or mother could survive childbirth at that point.

Culture

Unlike the primitive primates and early hominids, *Homo sapiens* babies were born with a soft spot on top of their skulls where the bone had not yet finished growing together (this is still true of human babies today). They were totally helpless and dependent on their mothers, and could not take care of themselves for several years. Unlike other animals, which were born with all kinds of survival instincts, these hominid babies were given very few patterns of instinctive behavior from their DNA. Their neocortex was almost completely blank—but it had a tremendous capacity to learn.

In fact, hominid brains had evolved to be so large and complex that they could hold more separate bits of information than all the countless molecules of DNA. These brains could (and still can) hold the equivalent of hundreds of thousands of books full of knowledge.

For eons, all living things had survived because of the instructions coded in their DNA. This was still true of *Homo sapiens* to some degree, but they had something else to help them survive: the wisdom passed down to each generation by word of mouth. This is called **culture**.

During their long childhood, hominid children depended on their parents and other members of the group and tribe to pass along all the know-how that had been collected by previous generations: how to get food, how to make clothes, how to start fires, how to talk, how to find shelter, how to make tools and weapons, how to avoid certain animals, and so on. With each generation, the amount of culture passed on to children grew a little larger as hominids improved and expanded the culture that had been passed to them.

This process is called **cultural evolution**. It's different from **biological evolution** (the slow changes in living bodies by natural selection), and it happens a lot faster. When hominids made an important invention or discovery (how to use fire, for example), they didn't have to wait thousands of generations for the idea to spread to future generations via DNA; they simply passed the message along by word of mouth. It spread to thousands of hominids in a matter of years, and became part of the culture passed down to each new generation of children.

Over the years, culture became more and more important to the survival of *Homo sapiens*. Imagine what would have happened if young children had been abandoned by their families before being taught how to light fires, hunt animals, and so on. Most of them would very quickly have starved to death or been gobbled up by predators.

The Ice Ages

Around the time that *Homo sapiens* evolved, the first of several great ice ages began. The Earth cooled down and snow and ice spread over large parts of Europe and Asia, not just in the winter but all the time. Most of the animals in the northern parts of the world froze to death. Only a few species survived because of lucky DNA changes that gave them thicker fur and the ability to hibernate underground during the coldest months. Other animals, like caribou and reindeer, collected in large herds and migrated from place to place looking for patches of vegetation to eat.

The hominids who were caught in the coldest parts of the world during the ice ages had a very hard time surviving. Despite all their clever inventions, many hominids froze and starved to death. During this period, hominids hunted the really big mammals like **mammoths**, which looked like hairy elephants. This meant working in large hunting groups and using new tactics. One trick was to frighten the animal into jumping off a cliff, and then cutting up the dead body at the bottom. Hominids divided up the meat among the hunters' groups and tried to make it last for a long time, but often they went hungry. Life during the ice ages was a continual struggle, with starvation a constant threat.

Some hominids watched large herds of caribou and reindeer migrating from place to place and had an idea: Why not travel with the animals, killing only a few at a time so that there was always plenty of meat? Some groups of hominids began to follow the wandering herds wherever they went. The herd was like a moving supply of meat, and these hominids found ways of using every part of the caribou or reindeer they killed: The skins could be made into clothes and tents, the bones into knives, the antlers into tools, and so forth. Hominids who developed this life of constantly moving from place to place are called **nomads**.

As *Homo sapiens* spread around Europe and Asia and struggled to survive, several **subspecies** evolved. Scientists have found fossils of one kind of hominid named ***Homo neanderthalensis*** whose brains were actually bigger than those of most modern humans. They also had more massive bodies, and apparently were well adapted to living in the very cold conditions of the ice ages.

Scientists have found that the bones of these hominids often have rocks carefully piled around them. This indicates that Neanderthals took great care in burying members of their group when they died. At one burial site, traces of pollen were found around the bones. Other hominids must have brought flowers and laid them around the grave. Obviously these hominids were doing a lot of thinking about what happened after death.

Hominids of several subspecies also began to decorate their tools and weapons in ways that went beyond pure function. This was the beginning of art. Later on, some hominids in Europe painted animals, hunters, and other pictures on the walls of caves. The interesting thing is that these paintings were not done in the caves in which hominids ate and slept; the artists did their work in special caves that were very hard to get into. Hominids may have gone to these secret places before a hunt and looked at the paintings to psych themselves up for the danger and excitement of the kill—or perhaps after the hunt to pay homage to the spirits of the animals whose bodies gave them life.

The paintings, decorations, and other artwork of these hominids show that they had a real sense of beauty along with their awareness of death. Perhaps these two things together spurred the creativity of early artists who wanted to leave their mark on the world before they died. Perhaps their works of art were a way of saying to future generations, "Here I am; I made this. Remember me!"

Homo sapiens sapiens

About 50,000 years ago, a subspecies of *Homo sapiens* had evolved which scientists call ***Homo sapiens sapiens***. These creatures had bodies just like those of all humans on Earth today, and we are all descended from them. People used to think that the different races of humans were descended from different subspecies of hominids; but scientists now know (based on a careful study of the chemicals and DNA messages inside human bodies) that all races are members of only one subspecies—*Homo sapiens sapiens*.

Modern humans probably evolved in the Middle East, near the eastern end of the Mediterranean Sea, and gradually spread outward. Over thousands of years they moved into Europe, Asia, and Africa, across the narrow land bridge that at that time connected Asia with North America, into South America, and by primitive boats to Australia and the countless islands around the world.

As they spread, modern humans may have interbred with, and certainly competed against and slowly replaced, the earlier hominids, including the Neanderthals (whose bodies were too specifically adapted to ice-age conditions). Eventually humans were the only creatures of their kind. They survived and spread because they were the most intelligent, skillful, and adaptable creature on Earth.

Homo sapiens sapiens probably evolved in the Middle East and spread in all directions until he lived in most parts of the world.

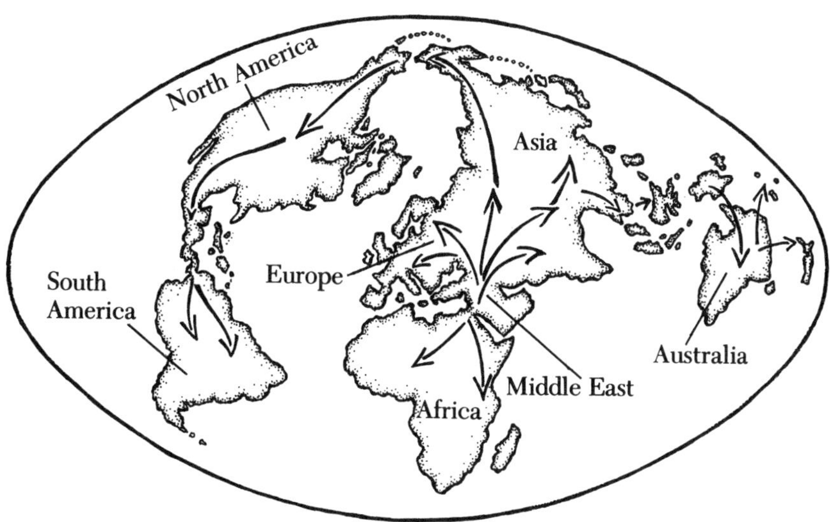

10

Human Differences

If all humans are part of one sub-species, **Homo sapiens sapiens,** why are we so different from one another now? To answer this question, we have to backtrack a little. As hominids spread out, they lived in a variety of climates: hot deserts, thick jungles, open grasslands, temperate forests, and the frigid, snow-covered land of the north. In each different environment, hominids had to change their culture and tools and weapons to survive. Over the years they invented bows and arrows, spears, harpoons, fish hooks, sleds, and whatever else would help them get food and stay alive.

Hominid bodies also went through some minor changes as they moved to different parts of the world. In the cold northern regions, people with heavier bodies were able to retain heat and go longer without food, which was important to survival. Those who happened to have the DNA code for stocky bodies tended to survive and pass that trait to their children, until most hominids in the coldest parts of the world were stocky.

In the hot regions close to the equator, the exact opposite was true: People with slim bodies and long limbs could more easily get rid of excess body heat. So those who happened to have the DNA code for thinness were more likely to survive and pass the trait down to future generations.

The different skin colors of humans around the world

evolved for the same reasons. Originally, a certain kind of skin was an advantage to surviving in that particular environment. The first hominids were covered with thick hair. This protected their skin from the rays of the sun. But over time, some hominids happened to have thinner, finer hair and millions of pores in their skin. These allowed them to sweat from every part of their bodies. Thinner hair and pores were an advantage in one way—they allowed those hominids to work harder and run farther in hot places—but a disadvantage in another way—the hominids' skin was exposed to the burning rays of the sun.

Once again, DNA variations and mutations helped evolution along. Some hominids happened to have a protective brown substance called **melanin** in their skin. It soaked up sunlight and kept the skin from getting burned. Over the years, these three traits evolved together—because hominids with thin hair, millions of pores, and melanin survived. Eventually, most hominids in hot parts of the world had dark brown skin.

Some of these hominids slowly migrated north to parts of Asia and Europe, where the sun's rays were weaker, the days were shorter, and the winters were longer. Here the skin was exposed to much less sunlight. Dark skin was not necessary to survival—in fact, the reverse became true. Hominids with lots of melanin in their skin began to get sick.

The problem was this: The sun was their main means of making **vitamin D**, which is manufactured in skin that is struck by sunlight. The melanin in their skin was blocking the sunlight they needed to make *enough* of this important substance. The result was a vitamin deficiency that caused a disease called **rickets**, which weakened bones and caused mothers to die in childbirth. Modern humans also need vitamin D, but we get ours from milk, fish, and other foods which our ancestors hadn't yet begun to eat.

Obviously, hominids with dark-brown skin didn't last too long in cooler parts of the world. But as we know, no two children are born exactly the same. Even within the same family, some were born with lighter skin that contained less melanin. Any hominids with this trait had a better chance of surviving in the north, because the weak sunlight could get through their skin and make vitamin D. Over the generations, light-skinned hominids survived and spread, and rickets was no longer a problem for them. Many hominids died in the process, but the species slowly evolved to survive in the new cooler environment.

Modern Races

As *Homo sapiens sapiens* evolved and spread south into Africa and north into Europe and Asia, skin color went through these changes. This resulted in the modern races that we know as Negro and Caucasian ("black" and "white"), and many other racial groups and subgroups in between. Humans who lived in hot parts of Asia (Orientals) evolved with lighter, yellowish skin that had different properties from the skin of Negroes and Caucasians: It could reflect the burning rays of the sun, but didn't block out the rays that made vitamin D.

As Orientals moved south through the Americas, they evolved with reddish-brown skin, while those who crossed from Asia to Australia evolved with dark brown skin similar to that of African Negroes.

These changes in skin color didn't make the various races of humans into separate species (they could still interbreed and were still basically the same inside) or even into separate subspecies. But they did limit the areas of the world in which they could survive. Dark-skinned people couldn't live too far from the equator or they would get rickets, and light-skinned people couldn't live too close to the equator or they would get sunburned (and also get overdoses of vitamin D, which caused a different kind of illness).

For a while, these different races were "trapped" in their general environments, in the same way that animals were locked into the environments for which their bodies had evolved. But soon humans found ways to free themselves from the geographical restrictions of skin color. You can probably guess what some of these were.

Other Differences

Skin color was only one of the variations among humans living in different parts of the world. There were many others. Melanin was present in the eyes and hair too. Different amounts of melanin produced black, brown, and blond hair and many colors of eyes, including light blue, green, gray, brown, and black.

There were also variations in hair texture, body shape, height, head size, blood type, and in the shapes of eyes, noses, ears, cheeks, teeth, lips, and so on. The constant shuffling and reshuffling of DNA messages with each generation produced a tremendous variety in human appearance.

People in different parts of the world had very different ideas about what made a person attractive. In each area, those who were thought to be attractive were sought after as mates; they tended to have more babies than those who were considered unattractive. In this way, the attractive traits, whatever they happened to be in each area, were passed along to future generations and spread more widely in the tribe. Humans were choosing which characteristics would become dominant in their area. This process is called **social selection**.

It's important to remember, though, that all these differences between groups of humans were only skin deep. Scientists have studied the chemicals, brains, hearts, bones, muscles, and blood of humans from every racial group in the world, and have found that inside there are no significant differences.

In another sense, though, humans aren't the same at all. Even though we're made of the same chemicals, some individuals are more intelligent, athletic, skillful, or resourceful than others. Each of us has many different strengths and weaknesses. How can this happen if we are all the same inside? There are two explanations.

First, all children receive new combinations of DNA from their parents. With each generation, the DNA codes are shuffled like cards. Some people happen to be dealt better hands than others; they inherit traits that make them better athletes, better inventors, better artists, and so on than other people, including some of their own brothers and sisters. These abilities are spread pretty evenly around the races and groups of the world, so a person's inherited abilities are largely a matter of luck.

Second, the way humans are treated as children has a big effect on what they can do later on. If children don't get enough to eat and aren't taught necessary skills, they will not be as strong and knowledgeable and able to cope with the world as children who are well fed and well educated.

For years, people have debated about which of these two factors is more important. Some say that we inherit most of our abilities and weaknesses; others say that our environment as children and adults explains the way we turn out. This debate will go on for years, but most scientists now think that human differences are explained by both heredity and environment.

11

Herding, Fishing, and Farming

About 12,000 years ago, the last of the great ice ages finally ended. The climates of Europe and Asia and North America warmed up, and most of the great sheets of ice melted. Green plants flourished and great forests spread through the northern parts of the world. The water from all that melting ice trickled into the oceans, and slowly the water level rose until it was 400 feet higher than it had been during the ice ages. This flooded large areas of dry land near the coasts and forced humans and animals to retreat to higher ground.

In the north, finding food became much easier for humans with the coming of warmer weather. They were able to give up the hard life of hunting big game and following herds of caribou and reindeer. One new way of getting food was to round up and tend small herds of wild goats, sheep, or cattle. People who became herders could drink milk from the female animals and kill one of their herd for meat anytime they wanted to eat. By allowing their herds to reproduce, humans could grow their own meat supply; if they took good care of their animals and had good luck, there was plenty of food. Some humans also tamed wild dogs, and used them to control their herds and protect them from predatory animals.

The problem with keeping a herd of sheep or goats or cattle

was that after a few weeks in one place, the animals had chewed up all the vegetation and had nothing left to eat. The only way to keep the herd alive was to move on to another place with greener pastures. So herders were never able to settle down and build permanent houses or towns; like their ancestors for countless generations, they were nomads, constantly on the move to assure themselves a good supply of food.

After a while, the animals in these herds were **domesticated**; they were completely dependent on humans to drive them from place to place, get them across rivers and mountains, protect them from wild animals, and make sure they could get enough to eat. These animals needed human care as much as humans needed the animals' milk and meat; they were mutually dependent.

There was an important difference between herders and humans who hunted and gathered or followed wild caribou. Herders actually changed the natural habits of several animals to suit human needs. With the invention of herding, humans had taken a step toward controlling nature, changing the world around them to suit their purposes and help their survival.

Population Problems

Some humans became expert fishermen. In a few places they were able to catch enough fish to feed a small population of people for a long time. In these places the river or lake brought food to the people, and they didn't have to keep moving. For the first time it was possible to build houses and settle down. The remains of a few small fishing villages have been found on the banks of lakes and rivers in Europe, one with about fifty houses.

But these villages couldn't be much bigger than this because early humans couldn't catch enough fish to support a larger population. For many more years, humans around the world were very spread out and continued to live in small groups; most of them were still nomads, constantly moving from place to place to feed their herds or find new territory for hunting and gathering.

Although each group of humans was quite small, the total number of humans kept increasing. In the years immediately following the end of the last ice age, the human population of the world grew to about 10 million. In some areas where the climate was warm and there was lots of water and vegetation, humans reproduced so rapidly that it started getting crowded. People began to bump into each other's food-gathering and grazing territory, and there wasn't enough food to go around.

As people in crowded areas looked around for new sources of food, they noticed many edible plants that had sprung up since the end of the last ice age; one of them was wild wheat. Some people discovered that if they picked wheat, ground up the kernels, mixed them into a dough with water, and cooked the dough over a fire, they got a nutritious new food—bread. This was such a good idea that it spread quickly, and over the years more and more people added different kinds of bread to their diet.

Agriculture

By this time, people in many parts of the world probably knew that the sun and the presence of water made plants grow. While humans couldn't control the sun, they could divert water from rivers and irrigate fields of wild wheat to make them grow better and produce more bread.

Then it occurred to some people that they didn't have to roam around looking for fields of wild wheat; they could plant the seeds and grow their own crops wherever they would grow. People probably made this discovery accidentally when they spilled some seeds on the ground and noticed that little plants sprang up several days later. They began to plant lots of seeds, and after several months of irrigation and growth, they harvested their own crop of wheat.

This deliberate planting and harvesting is called **agriculture** or farming. The idea was one of the most brilliant and important in human history. Scientists think that farming was probably invented independently in several different parts of the world at different times, but the first place that humans became farmers was almost certainly in the Middle East, between the Tigris and Euphrates rivers. This area has been called the Fertile Crescent because of its new-moon shape and the fact that there was enough warm sunshine, rich soil, and water for crops to grow easily.

As the idea of agriculture spread around the Middle East, it had an enormous effect on the way people lived. Farmers had to settle down in one place and wait for the seeds to grow into plants that they could harvest. Agriculture forced these humans to give up their nomadic way of life.

It also solved the food shortage in the Middle East and other crowded places. As farmers became experienced, they found that one field could supply enough food for more than just the immediate family group; a number of fields could feed a fairly large population. Agriculture used less land to produce food than herding or hunting and gathering, and therefore made it possible for people to live closer together. According to one scientist, this is the amount of land needed to feed a group of humans with each of the methods used so far:

Gathering and hunting	1,000 acres
Herding	100 acres
Agriculture	5 acres

Now that farmers could feed many more people within a small area, people could begin to live in villages, towns, and eventually cities.

Astronomy and Religion

To survive as farmers, people had to understand the seasons; otherwise they wouldn't know what time of year to plant and when to harvest their crops. Over the eons, many people may have noticed that the sun, moon, and stars moved across the sky on regular schedules. The movements of heavenly bodies could be very helpful to farmers, and those who could predict the seasons by watching the sky—the first **astronomers**—were very important people.

In many cultures, astronomy was very closely linked to religion (the worship of gods) because the heavens filled people with such a sense of wonder. Most people came to believe that the Earth and sky were created and controlled by all-powerful gods, and different cultures created different rituals to worship their gods.

Religions around the world were very different, but they all helped people in the same ways: They explained the natural forces people saw around them, told people how the universe had begun and where humans came from, gave them some hope for a life after death, and gave people a feeling that their lives had some meaning. Earthquakes, thunderstorms, volcanoes, hurricanes, diseases, and other natural forces had always frightened humans and made them feel small and powerless; religions explained all these phenomena as the work of powerful gods who were angry, jealous, vengeful, or just doing their thing. Religions also provided rules which told people how to behave in their daily lives. By worshipping their gods and following these rules, people felt that the world made sense.

Agriculture Improves

Over the years, farmers found ways to produce more food with less work. They learned how to use animals to pull plows; they planted other crops, including barley, corn, vegetables, and grass to feed their domesticated animals; and they selected the

Over the years, humans developed the art of farming and began to live closer together in larger and larger communities.

seeds of their best plants to sow for the next crop, thus improving the size and yield of each year's harvest. As farmers grew more food than their village needed to eat, they were able to trade with nearby villages and store some food for the future. Having some surplus (extra) food on hand allowed people to escape some of the day-to-day worries about having enough to eat, and was a big change from the life of earlier humans, who seldom looked further ahead than their next meal.

Of course farming communities had their problems. There were times when there wasn't enough rain, when insects ate the crops, when rivers overflowed their banks and washed away the precious topsoil, and other disasters. But most farmers survived these bad times and continued to develop and improve the art of agriculture. Farming was such a good idea that it spread around the world. Over the next few thousand years, more and more people began to plant crops and settle down in villages and towns. After a while there were very few nomads and hunter-gatherers left.

Humans had taken a big step; instead of adapting to fit into the environment, they were changing the environment to suit their needs. Previous ways of life had kept groups of humans fairly small and their food gathering in balance with nature. Now all that had begun to change.

12

Civilization

Following the invention of agriculture, villages and towns got bigger, the first cities were built, and the pace of invention speeded up dramatically. A whole new series of ideas sprang up to help farmers grow their crops and to make people's lives easier and better. Over the years, resourceful people figured out how to:

- divert great rivers to irrigate larger fields
- shape clay into bowls and pots and harden them in fires
- carry heavy loads on rollers
- use carts with wheels and axles
- dig wells and pull water up with ropes and pulleys
- melt copper to make tools, weapons, and ornaments
- mix copper and tin to make a harder metal called bronze
- use iron and harden it into steel
- build boats to carry food and other goods
- count and keep track of things by making marks in clay or stone
- write down symbols to represent various words and ideas, first in stone and clay, later on paper
- tame and ride horses and camels
- make cloth from sheep's wool and cotton, and stitch it into clothes

- build bigger and fancier houses, public buildings, and places of worship
- create more elaborate and beautiful art, including carvings, statues, and paintings

All this and much more is what we call civilization.

In the villages and towns and cities, there was enough of a food surplus so that not everyone had to be a farmer. People began to specialize in different jobs. Some raised animals, some built houses, some made plows, some fixed carts, some dug wells, some made clothes, and so on. This meant that each family group was no longer self-sufficient; people needed to trade with other people to get what they needed to survive. This exchange of goods and services (I'll give you some milk if you'll fix my roof) is called **barter**. As time went by, people began to use shells, stones, or precious metals to represent certain amounts of goods and services, in the same way that money is used today.

Laws and Leaders

As people collected more possessions, theft became more of a problem. Some people had always stolen things they hadn't worked or paid for. But it was harder to catch them in a large town or city than it had been in the small groups of nomads or hunter-gatherers.

There were also more arguments in crowded communities; people disagreed about land, water, lovers, husbands, wives, bartering, money, religion, and so on. Unless there were laws (which were often part of religion), and unless there were strong leaders and police officers to enforce the laws, living in large communities could be violent and chaotic.

Another problem in ancient communities was that diseases were spread by insects and rats, killing many humans and domesticated animals. For a long time, people didn't understand what caused diseases and how they spread, and had no way to control them. Sickness and early death were very common. Sometimes whole communities were wiped out.

Farming communities were also afflicted by wandering tribes of nomads who stole the wheat, milk, animals, and all the other things farmers had worked so hard to produce. Civilized people began to build walls around their communities and close their gates at night. They also made weapons and got together to defend themselves against these organized thieves. The first walled city in the world was probably Jericho, which was built in the Middle East about 8,000 years ago.

It wasn't easy to get people organized to build walls and fight invading nomads. But some people were natural leaders and exerted tremendous power over their followers. Over the years, many people became dependent on their leaders to provide protection, settle arguments, keep order, make laws, and tell them what gods to believe in. In return, these strong leaders usually asked their people to pay taxes in the form of produce or money. Some rulers used the taxes to build themselves up into extremely wealthy people.

In the days when humans were hunter-gatherers and nomads, it had been impossible for one leader to have this kind of control over large numbers of fellow humans. Groups were small and very spread out. Possessions were minimal—just what a person could conveniently carry from one campsite to the next. But as towns grew into cities and thousands of people lived on small areas of land, a ruler could get an iron grip on the lives of thousands of people.

Some rulers were fair and just. But in many cases, all this power corrupted leaders. They got carried away and grabbed more and more wealth and territory, forgetting that their original job was to govern and protect their people. The power-hungry leaders made themselves into pharaohs, emperors, kings, and queens, formed vast empires, made war on neighboring empires, and passed their power down to their children.

Many people in the early civilizations fell under the spell of these exciting leaders, and followed them into battle against other humans. If you read the history of the first civilizations (Sumer, Egypt, Assyria, Persia, and others), you will notice that most of the recorded story of humans in this period is the story of one war after another. Rulers sent their armies to capture more land and put more people under their rule, and thousands and thousands of people were killed or forced to work as slaves. Those who wanted to live in peace were seldom influential, and didn't find their way into many history books.

As conquering armies traveled around, they brought new ideas from place to place. This speeded the growth of human learning. Under some rulers, people put up spectacular buildings and built roads and bridges to make travel easier. Many empires encouraged artists and thinkers, produced countless beautiful works of art, and began to develop mathematics and science. The civilizations of the Egyptians, Hebrews, Greeks, Romans, and Arabs were among those that flourished in this period and have greatly influenced Western lives. There were also major civilizations in China, Africa, and the Americas.

The early civilizations recorded their ideas and history in clay tablets, on carved stones, and on paper, and passed a great deal of their knowledge on to future generations. The invention of spoken language by hominids millions of years before was the beginning of culture. Now humans could preserve their ideas, and the amount of human knowledge was no longer limited to what each person could remember. Written ideas could be passed around to many more people, and it became possible to pass on a far greater body of knowledge to future generations.

The Renaissance

There isn't room in this book to go into the details of human history over the next few thousand years. If you're interested, you can read history books to learn more about the civilizations, religions, wars, the "Dark Ages," the formation of modern countries, and the development of art during these years. We're going to skip ahead to the **Renaissance**, only about 600 years ago, when there was a "rebirth" of ideas and art in the countries of western Europe. Many of the ideas that were rediscovered during this period came from the ancient civilizations of Greece and Rome thousands of years before.

At the time of the Renaissance, many people in Europe dreamed of traveling to far-off places. Some felt crowded in Europe and wanted more elbow room. Others wanted adventure and hoped to make themselves rich. But traveling by land was hard and dangerous, and sailing in boats seemed even worse. People feared storms and sea monsters, and thought that if they sailed too far out to sea, they would fall off the edge of the world. This was because most people believed that the world was flat, with the moon and sun and stars moving across a dome high over their heads. Some people believed that the whole universe rested on the back of an enormous turtle.

But over the years, people began to wonder if this was really true. They noticed that when a ship sailed out to sea, it didn't just get smaller in the distance; it actually seemed to go down into the ocean. If the world was flat, why would that happen? There were other questions: If a ship sailed off the edge of the world, where would it go? What was the turtle standing on? And what was on the other side of the dome above the world?

During the Renaissance, people rediscovered a theory that had been developed in ancient Greece, about 1,700 years before. The idea was that the Earth was shaped like a ball. For many people this was hard to believe; but for the European sailors who wanted to explore what was over the horizon, it was a piece of good news. If the theory was true, it meant that they would not fall off the edge of the world. What's more, it meant,

Some early people thought the world was flat and rested on the back of an enormous turtle. They were afraid that if they sailed too far out to sea, they would fall off the edge.

if they kept sailing in one direction, that they would come back to the place where they had started.

In 1492, a sailor named Christopher Columbus caused a sensation. He sailed across the Atlantic Ocean and back. Europeans realized that they could take their small wooden sailing ships just about anywhere in the world. Soon, other explorers set out on longer and longer expeditions.

Europeans weren't the first people to make long sea voyages. Polynesians had crossed parts of the Pacific Ocean and some Africans may have crossed the Atlantic long before 1492. Norse explorers had settled the northern coast of America 500 years earlier. But the Europeans took exploration a step further. They began to colonize the places they "discovered," usually pushing aside the people who had been living there. Soon thousands of Europeans moved to the Americas, Africa, Asia, and Australia and set up colonies. Then the Europeans began to bring Africans across the Atlantic to work as slaves in North and South America.

As more and more people traveled around the world, the distribution of races and groups that had evolved thousands of years before was completely changed. People were no longer limited by their skin color; light-skinned people could live in the hot sun near the equator if they wore clothes and hats. And dark-skinned people could live far from the equator if they ate food that contained enough vitamin D.

Copernicus

While all this was going on, a great debate was raging, back in Europe, about the Earth's place in the universe. Most people got used to the idea that the Earth was round; but they still believed that the Earth was the center of the universe—that the sun and moon and stars revolved around it.

Then in 1543, a scientist named Copernicus shocked the

world with a new theory. After years of watching the sky, he announced that the Earth was not the center of the universe. In fact, said Copernicus, the Earth and several other planets were in orbit around the sun, which he was convinced was the true center of the universe.

This new theory made people dizzy. They found it very upsetting to hear that the Earth was not the center of the universe and most of them didn't want to hear it. Many religious people were furious about the new theory, and they attacked Copernicus and anyone who supported his ideas. Some scientists were actually burned at the stake for saying that the Earth was not the center of the universe.

In spite of this kind of treatment, scientists kept up their work, and over the years more and more people got used to the idea that the Earth was just a small planet spinning around the sun.

13

Industry and Technology

Beginning around 1760, there was another profound change in human history. It was called the **Industrial Revolution**. Up to this point, most people lived in villages and towns surrounded by fields. There were few large cities. But then a series of inventions—among them the steam engine, the railroad, and mass production—turned all that upside down.

Many factory jobs were created, and millions of people moved from farms to new cities to work in industries making machines, clothes, shoes, guns, ships, and countless other products. The countries that industrialized first (England, Germany, France, the United States, and a few others) got a head start and quickly became the richest and most powerful countries in the world. They exploited their own natural resources and those of the poorer countries, and built bigger factories, bigger cities, bigger armies and navies, and bigger empires.

Because they were richer and more technologically advanced, most people in these countries came to believe that they were better, in all senses, than the people in the poorer countries, and tried to convert the "savages" to European religions and customs. They also brought modern medicines to the poorer countries and showed people how to cure and prevent many terrible diseases, which cut down the death rate. But for a variety of reasons, people in the poorer countries did not limit the number of babies that were born. The result was a tremendous increase in the populations of these countries, which meant more and more hungry stomachs to feed.

After the Industrial Revolution, there was a stream of discoveries and inventions in science and medicine. This was called the **Technological Revolution**. Doctors learned how to control germs that had disfigured and killed humans for thousands of years. They also began to operate successfully on living human bodies. In other fields, engineers built steel bridges, tunnels, and skyscrapers, and brought electricity into many people's homes. Scientists found ways of sending radio and television signals through the air so that millions of people could enjoy music and entertainment which once had been available only to the very rich. Communication around the world improved so dramatically, the size of the planet seemed to shrink. Humans launched rockets that escaped the Earth's gravity and explored the solar system. Scientists also began to put together a completely new story of how life in the universe began.

Outer Space

As scientists continued to peer through more and more powerful telescopes, they slowly realized that the sun was not the center of the universe (as Copernicus had believed). They found that the sun was only one of billions of stars in the Milky Way galaxy. Then scientists developed even more powerful telescopes, and looked beyond our galaxy and deep into space. Many of the tiny pinpricks of light that looked like stars turned out to be distant galaxies. Each galaxy contained billions of individual stars. People realized that our Milky Way was only one of billions of galaxies in the universe.

Then a scientist named Edwin Hubble found evidence that the galaxies were not fixed in position, but were flying outward into space at incredible speed. This discovery led scientists to conclude that everything in the universe was once squeezed together in one incredibly dense ball which exploded 15 billion years ago in the Big Bang.

Could there be life on other planets or moons in the universe? From what we have learned about the way life evolved on Earth, it's entirely possible that the same process happened elsewhere. All that is necessary are certain atoms (which are created every time a supernova happens), a planet that is the right distance from a star so that it's not too hot and not too cold, and a good many years for the chemicals to be formed and mix with each other until self-reproducing molecules and cells are formed. Some scientists think these conditions exist on many planets in the universe, and that life as complicated as that on the planet Earth (and maybe even more technologically advanced) exists throughout the galaxies.

But if life does exist on other planets, it probably doesn't look anything like what we see around us on Earth. Remember why life on this planet looks the way it does? A long series of accidental mutations and DNA changes helped living things fit into the particular environment in which they were growing. If life evolved on another planet, the environment there was probably not the same, which would mean life would be quite different from what we see on Earth. We might not even recognize the creatures from another planet as being alive.

As you sit here thinking about life on other planets, there may be intelligent creatures on another planet far away reading a book similar to this one and wondering the same thing about us. They may even have gotten to the stage of building space rockets and exploring the galaxies around them.

But the trouble with visiting other solar systems is that the distances are so enormous. The star nearest to us, after our sun, is Alpha Centauri, and it is 24,000,000,000,000 miles away. It would take a very fast rocket hundreds of years to travel there and back, and much longer to reach other solar systems. Another problem is that there is a limit on how fast a spaceship can travel. According to Albert Einstein, one of the most brilliant scientists of all time, nothing can ever travel faster than the speed of light (186,283 miles per second), which takes 4 years just to get to Alpha Centauri.

A quicker way of finding out whether there is intelligent life on other planets is to point very sensitive radio atennae into the sky and listen for signs of life from civilizations that might have learned how to use radio waves. Since a radio signal travels at about the speed of light, it can cover the vast distances between solar systems much faster than a rocket; but even so, a signal from a distant planet might take many, many years to reach us. Scientists have been listening through their antennae for several years. So far they have picked up no signs of life from outer space.

Modern Problems

If we could make contact with an advanced civilization on another planet that could be a real plus. Maybe the creatures we reach could tell us how they handled the problems they came across in their development and give us a little advice with ours. We could use it. In the last 12,000 years, humans on Earth have gone from caves to skyscrapers, from stone tools to laser beams, from bows and arrows to machine guns and atomic bombs, from ox power to electricity, from smoke signals to telephones and radios, and from ox carts to space rockets. We are civilized. Yet we are still facing four problems that threaten the existence of *all* life on Earth.

1. Overpopulation The invention of agriculture made people think they could feed any number of hungry stomachs. But we have reached the limit in many parts of the world. Before farming, there were about 10 million humans on the planet Earth; now there are 400 times that many—about 4 billion people—two thirds of whom don't have enough food. Every day about 150,000 more people are born than die, which is like adding a good-sized city to the world's population every 24 hours.

If people keep reproducing at the present rate, there will be terrible overcrowding and mass starvation in many parts of the world, especially in the poor countries that have the highest birthrates and the least food. The development of effective methods of birth control in the last few decades gives some reason for hope. The richest countries have almost stopped their population growth. But some religions have strong objections to artificial birth control, and the poorest countries are only beginning to limit their population growth. Some people worry that it may be too late to avoid disaster.

2. *Pollution* Another major problem is the way we humans are upsetting the **ecology** of the Earth—the delicate balance of air, water, land, and life that makes our planet livable. By burning wood, coal, and oil, cutting down countless trees, digging up the earth, dumping wastes, and releasing certain harmful gases into the atmosphere, we have begun to affect the web of life in dangerous ways. For example, some gases from spray cans, jet airplanes, and other human sources are thinning out the ozone layer that protects us from the sun's deadly ultraviolet rays. If this continues, more of these rays will penetrate the atmosphere and have a destructive effect on many living things. Unless we find ways to stop polluting the environment, we may endanger all life on Earth.

3. *Nuclear Weapons* Since the development of the atomic bomb in the 1940s, several countries have built nuclear weapons capable of destroying entire cities and poisoning the areas around them for years after the bombs explode. Because of fear and suspicion between these countries, nuclear weapons in missiles, planes, and submarines are ready to be launched at a moment's notice. If there were a nuclear war, hundreds of millions of people would be killed. The survivors would return to a very primitive existence. Some leaders are trying hard to create more friendly relations and cut back on the number of bombs, but it is a very slow and difficult process.

4. Poverty Since the Industrial Revolution two centuries ago, an enormous gap has opened up between the rich and poor countries of the world. In the industrialized nations there is enough food, most people live in reasonable comfort, and population growth is under control. But in the poor countries millions of people are starving or leading miserable lives. The population is increasing so fast that things are getting worse every day. People in the rich nations consume much of the world's energy and food; millions of people in the poor countries worry every day whether they will get enough to eat.

Can we solve the dangerous problems of overpopulation, pollution, nuclear weapons, and poverty? Or will humans—the most skillful and adaptable creatures ever to live on Earth—drive themselves into extinction by creating an environment in which they cannot survive? Scientists estimate that of all the species that have lived on the Earth since life began, 99% are now extinct. Will *Homo sapiens sapiens* remain part of the 1% of survivors? Or will our species's time on the planet be but a brief sideshow when compared to successfully adapted animals like fish, reptiles, and insects that live in harmony with nature?

The real question is whether we have the courage and intelligence to find solutions that will allow us and our civilization to survive. It's no use waiting to get ideas from creatures from outer space. Their suggestions may come too late. Within the next few decades—well within your lifetime—we will all have to deal with these problems ourselves.

14

From the Big Bang to You

As you sit reading this book, you are a living, breathing summary of the entire story of the universe. The fact that you know how to read is a reflection of the thousands of years it has taken humans to develop the alphabet, learn how to read and write, and pass that knowledge down to you. The book you are holding is made possible by hundreds of years of technology—paper mills, typewriters, electricity, printing presses, binding machines, trucks, trains, etc.—which put the finished product into your hands. And the ideas you have been reading about in this book are the product of many years of scientific exploration into the life of the universe.

As you read, your heart is quietly beating, your lungs are pulling in fresh air for your blood to circulate, your stomach is digesting, and your other organs are doing their jobs under the direction of your immensely complicated brain. Without any conscious effort from you, each of your 10 billion cells is doing its part to keep your body going according to the master plan in your DNA.

The DNA molecules that gave the instructions to make your body were formed at the beginning of your life, nine months before you were born, when one of your father's sperm cells fertilized one of your mother's egg cells. But was that the beginning of life for those two cells? Certainly not. Your mother's egg cell and your father's sperm cell were very much alive when they joined to begin your life. They were made inside your parents' bodies from other living cells, which grew from other living cells, which originally grew from the living egg and sperm cells of their parents, your grandparents. Their living cells originally grew from the living egg and sperm cells of their mothers and fathers (your great-grandparents), and so on back through the generations.

If you want to trace the life in your body back to its real beginning, you have to go back through the family tree of your ancestors, back thousands of years to the original *Homo sapiens sapiens*, back even further to the hominids, back through the primates, the mammals, the reptiles, the amphibians, the fish, the worms, the first eucaryotic cells, and finally to the first replicating cell in the ocean. The stream of life from the original living cell to you is continuous and unbroken. The life in your body has been going nonstop for 3½ billion years.

You are one of the outermost tips of one of the newest branches of the tree of life, directly related to all the other branches of living things on Earth. We all trace our roots back billions of years to the beginning of life in the primitive ocean, and from there to the amino acids and nucleotide bases that somehow formed the first living cell; from there to the molecules that hooked together in the primitive atmosphere; from there to the atoms that pulled together to form the Earth; from there to the supernova that fused those atoms together; from there to the hydrogen and helium atoms that formed early stars; from there to the tiny particles in space; and from there to the Big Bang that began the whole process. The raw materials in all our bodies date back 15 billion years to the very beginning of our universe.

Look at one of your hands and think of the journey the atoms in it have made so far.

And think of the journey they have yet to make.

Glossary

This section contains short definitions of words that are printed in **bold type** in the text. There's a pronunciation guide to the more difficult words. If you want more detailed and scientific definitions and more information, you should look at some of the books in the bibliography, use an encyclopedia, or go to the library and find other books.

agriculture: the deliberate planting, growing, and harvesting of plants by humans.

amino acids: (uh-*mee*-no a-sidz) complex molecules contained in all living things on Earth; amino acids are made of millions of hydrogen, carbon, nitrogen, and oxygen atoms hooked together in long chains. There are 20 different kinds of amino acids in living things.

amphibians: (am-*fib*-ee-uhnz) animals that live part of the time on land and part of the time in the water; young amphibians go through a fishlike stage before growing legs and moving onto land for most of their food.

asteroids: (*as*-ter-oydz) small chunks of matter in space; in our solar system, there is a belt of asteroids between Mars and Jupiter.

astronomer: a scientist who studies the stars and other heavenly bodies.

atom: the smallest unit into which things in the universe can be divided and still remain themselves. All atoms are made of the same basic particles—protons, neutrons, and electrons—but the number and arrangement of these building blocks determines the properties of atoms. There are over a hundred different kinds of atoms in the universe. A material made up of only one kind of atom is called an element; one made up of several different kinds is a compound.

***Australopithecus africanus*:** (aw-stray-lo-*pith*-eh-kus af-ri-*kan*-us) a hominid that lived in Africa and possibly in parts of Asia several million years ago and became extinct about 1½ million years ago; these hominids had slim bodies and grew to be about four feet tall.

***Australopithecus robustus*:** (aw-stray-lo-*pith*-eh-kus ro-*buhs*-tus) a hominid that lived in Africa and possibly in parts of Asia several million years ago and became extinct. These hominids were more heavyset than *Australopithecus africanus* and grew to be about five feet tall.

axis: the imaginary line through the center of a sphere (a planet or star or moon, for instance) around which it spins.

bacteria (germs): simple one-celled units of life that feed on other living or dead cells.

barter: the direct exchange of goods and services, without money changing hands (I'll give you some wheat if you dig me a well).

Big Bang: the gigantic explosion that was the birth of our universe between 10 and 20 billion years ago. Scientists know very little about what made the Big Bang happen, and nothing about what existed before it—but they have deduced that there *was* such an explosion from the fact that all galaxies are still flying outward now, and from faint background radiation from the explosion.

biological evolution: the slow changes in living bodies—by mutations, DNA recombinations, and natural selection—by which living things become better and better adapted to and by each environment.

birth canal (vagina): the passage in all female mammals, including humans, through which male sperm enter the female's body and through which babies are born.

cartilage: (*kahr*-ti-ledj) tough fibrous material inside animals' bodies that holds together tissue and muscles, but is not as hard as bone; some present-day animals like sharks have cartilage instead of bones, as did the earliest fish.

cell: the basic unit of life on Earth: a package of chemicals including amino acids and nucleotide bases that can soak up nutrients, grow, split, and pass the message of life on to future generations.

chlorophyll: (*klawr*-uh-fil) a chemical inside plant cells that allows them to soak up sunlight and make protein; this process is called photosynthesis.

chloroplast: (*klawr*-uh-plasts) chemicals inside modern plant cells that give them the ability to soak up sunlight and photosynthesize.

cold-blooded: in animals, having a body temperature that adjusts to the temperature outside; if it's cold outside, the body is cold; if it's hot, the body becomes hot. Fish, amphibians, and reptiles are cold-blooded.

cultural evolution: the process by which ideas are passed down, modified, and improved over the generations; this kind of evolution happens by word of mouth, and is much faster than biological evolution, which depends on changes in the DNA.

culture: the wisdom passed down to each new generation of humans by word of mouth or writing, as distinct from genetic information passed down by DNA.

DNA (deoxyribonucleic acid): (dee-*ahx*-ee-*ry*-bo-nyoo-*klee*-ik a-sid) a nucleic acid supermolecule present in all living cells that makes reproduction and life possible. DNA consists of four nucleotide bases hooked together in a twisting double chain that resembles a twisted rope ladder; scientists think that every "step" consists of chemical "words" that carry instructions on how the cell should build itself up and split. The DNA supermolecule can peel itself apart into two identical strands and then build each of these strands back into a double strand in a new cell, then repeat the process over and over.

domesticated: tamed (as with animals); made responsive to human commands and dependent on human help for survival.

double helix: the scientific term for the shape of the DNA molecule, that of a twisted rope ladder.

Earth: the third planet out from our star, the sun; about 93,000,000 miles away.

ecology: the balance and interaction of air, water, land, and life on the planet Earth, or in smaller areas, that has evolved over the last 4½ billion years.

electromagnetic force: one of the most basic forces in the universe; it pulls particles together to form atoms. Without electromagnetic force, the particles that formed after the Big Bang would have kept flying out into space.

electron: (ee-*lek*-trahn) one of the basic particles that make up atoms; electrons are found zooming around the center of each atom, held in their orbits by electromagnetic force.

emotions: instinctive feelings of love, hate, jealousy, anger, etc., found in humans and other primates, and to a lesser degree in other mammals.

eucaryotes: (yoo-*kar*-ee-ots) modern cells; eucaryotes contain a nucleus, which houses their DNA, and a variety of other subcells and chemicals.

evolution: the gradual change in living things as they become better and better adapted to their environment over the generations. Evolution happens gradually by natural selection, as those less able to survive die off, and those with advantages that help them survive keep reproducing and passing their traits along. The three key steps in evolution are: mutation, which produces a wide variety of types of animal or plant or cell; overpopulation, which happens to virtually all forms of life as they reproduce beyond the limits of the food supply or the climate; and natural selection, by which those most able to survive pass on their traits while the others die out.

extinct: completely died out; having no member of the species left.

fertilization: the moment when a male sperm cell meets a female egg cell; at this moment, single DNA strands of each cell are combined, and the growth of a new cell or organism begins.

flagella: (fluh-*jel*-uh) tiny spinners that attach themselves to the outside of many eucaryotic animal cells and give them the ability to move around.

flint: a kind of stone that can be chipped into sharp-edged tools and weapons and used to strike sparks to light a fire; flint was used extensively by early humans and hominids.

fossils: hardened remains of ancient life found in rocks; fossils are formed when dead animals or plants are buried in mud, which then dries and hardens into rock that preserves or replaces the harder parts of the animal's body.

fusion: (*fyoo*-zhuhn) the reaction within stars in which hydrogen atoms are joined to become helium (and in larger stars into other heavier atoms). In fusion, four hydrogen atoms are squeezed together under great heat and pressure to form one helium atom; the helium atom formed is lighter than the four hydrogen atoms that formed it, and the missing weight comes out of the reaction in the form of tremendous energy—light, heat, and radiation.

galaxy: a cluster of about 100,000,000,000 stars; there are about 100,000,000,000 galaxies in our universe, and they take a variety of shapes, including pinwheels, discs, and spheres. The word "galaxy" comes from the Greek word for milk, and that word was used because of the whitish appearance of clusters of billions of stars against the blackness of space.

gravity: one of the most basic forces in the universe; gravity pulls objects toward one another. The more massive an object is, the stronger its gravity becomes.

gut: the digestive system that takes food in at one end, soaks up nutrients in the middle, and pushes wastes out the other end. The gut first evolved in primitive worms, and has been used by all higher animals, including humans.

helium: (*hee*-lee-uhm) the second-smallest and -simplest kind of atom in the universe (hydrogen is the smallest); each atom of helium consists of two protons and two neutrons in the center, with two electrons spinning around them.

hominids: (*hahm*-i-nidz) the general term for the many species of ground-dwelling descendants of early primates as they evolved into human beings. *Homo habilis, Homo erectus, Australopithecus,* and *Homo neanderthalensis* were all hominids.

***Homo erectus*:** (*ho*-mo ee-*rek*-tus) a hominid that evolved from one branch of *Homo habilis* about 2 million years ago and became extinct about 500,000 years ago as one branch evolved into *Homo sapiens*.

***Homo habilis*:** (*ho*-mo ha-*bil*-is) a hominid with a highly developed brain and large body that scientists think was a direct ancestor of modern humans. *Homo habilis* lived about 3 million years ago and became extinct when one branch evolved into *Homo erectus*.

***Homo neanderthalensis*:** (nee-*an*-duhr-thawl-ensis) a subspecies of *Homo sapiens* that scientists think was not on the main line of descent from *Homo erectus* to modern humans;

Neanderthals were larger bodied and larger brained than most modern humans, but their bodies were too narrowly adapted to ice-age conditions, and they became extinct after the end of the last ice age.

***Homo sapiens*:** (*ho*-mo *sa*-pee-enz) the species of hominid that evolved about 500,000 years ago and spread to many parts of the world. One branch of *Homo sapiens* evolved into *Homo sapiens sapiens*, modern humans.

***Homo sapiens sapiens*:** (*ho*-mo *sa*-pee-enz *sa*-pee-enz) the subspecies of *Homo sapiens* of which modern humans are members; this subspecies evolved from *Homo sapiens* about 50,000 years ago, probably in the Middle East, and spread outward to all parts of the world.

hydrogen: the simplest and smallest atom in the universe, consisting of one proton in the center with one electron spinning around it, held together by electromagnetic force.

Industrial Revolution: the enormous change in certain societies brought about by inventions such as the steam engine, mass-production factories, and railroads, and made for the movement of millions of people from the countryside to newly built cities to work in factory or service jobs.

invertebrates: animals with no backbone or internal skeleton; many invertebrates (like snails, scorpions, and crabs) have hard exterior shells.

lava: melted rock that lies below the Earth's crust and sometimes surges out of volcanoes.

lemur: (*lee*-mur) one of the early primates; lemurs were small, mouselike creatures with a number of body adaptations that suited them to life in the trees. Their descendants are still alive today, and have evolved with somewhat larger bodies.

mammals: warm-blooded animals that evolved from one branch of the reptile family about 250 million years ago. Mammals are characterized by body hair and milk-producing glands in females (the word mammal comes from the Latin word *mamma* meaning breast). Mammals became the dominant animals on Earth after the extinction of the giant reptiles 65 million years ago.

mammoth: a large hairy animal related to the modern elephant that lived in cold parts of the world during the ice ages.

meiosis: (my-*o*-sis) the peeling apart of DNA into single strands for sexual reproduction; a single strand is in each male sperm and female egg cell, and they combine at the moment of fertilization to start the growth of a new cell or organism.

melanin: (*mel*-uh-nin) a brown chemical in skin that soaks up sunlight; if there is a lot of melanin in the skin (which makes it dark brown), most sunlight is blocked and the skin is not burned by prolonged exposure to the sun. Melanin is also present in and affects the color of the eyes and hair.

meteorite: (*mee*-tee-awr-yts) small chunks of matter with fiery tails that orbit many stars.

microspheres: very small spheres, such as the protocells.

Milky Way: the galaxy in which we are located. The Milky Way is pinwheel shaped, and the Earth is located on the outer fringes.

mitochondria: (my-to-*kahn*-dree-uh) tiny subcells inside eucaryotic animal cells that give them the ability to use oxygen.

mitosis: (my-*to*-sis) reproduction by splitting into two identical cells.

molars: flat chewing teeth that help mammals grind up their food before swallowing it.

molecules: (*mahl*-e-kyoolz) combinations of atoms that have specific properties; for instance, two hydrogen atoms and one oxygen atom combine to form one molecule of water. Some molecules are combinations of different kinds of atoms, others contain only one kind.

monogamous: (muh-*nahg*-uh-muhs) choosing one mate, having children, and staying with the same mate for a long time.

mutant: (*myoo*-tuhnt) a cell that results from a mutation in the parent cell; mutants are slightly different, and if they survive, they pass on that difference to their offspring.

mutation: (myoo-*tay*-shuhn) a small mix-up or mistake in the DNA as it divides and re-forms into new cells. The result of mutations is that the message contained in the DNA molecule is different, and the mutant cells are not the same as their parent cell.

mutually reinforcing: helping each other along; each contributing to the other's development and/or survival.

natural selection: the process by which the best-adapted forms of life survive and the least adapted die; natural selection is often called the survival of the fittest.

neocortex (or cerebral cortex): (nee-o-*kawr*-teks) the area of the human or other hominid brain that makes possible logical thought, planning for the future, and higher intelligence.

neutron: (*nyoo*-trahn) one of the basic particles that make up atoms; neutrons are found in the center of all atoms except hydrogen, which has only one proton and one electron.

Nobel Prize: one of the highest honors a scientist can achieve is this annual award in physics, chemistry, and medicine (prizes are also given in literature, economics, and contributions to world peace); the prize was established in the will of a Swedish chemist named Alfred Nobel in 1896.

nomads: people who are always on the move, whether with herds, following caribou or reindeer, or seeking food in a harsh environment.

nucleic acids: (nyoo-*klee*-ik a-sidz) very complex molecules made of various nucleotide bases; one kind of nucleic acid is DNA, the molecule which makes it possible for cells to reproduce themselves.

nucleotide bases: (*nyoo*-klee-o-tyd bay-siz) complex molecules contained in all living things; nucleotide bases are very important to reproduction, since four different bases form DNA, the supermolecule that makes life possible.

nucleus: (*nyoo*-klee-uhs) the control center in eucaryotic cells, containing the DNA.

omnivorous: (ahm-*niv*-o-ruhs) a diet consisting of both meat and plant food.

opposable thumb: in hominids, humans, and other primates, a thumb that can be wrapped around the side of a branch or rock or other object opposite from the other four fingers; having opposable thumbs gave these creatures a much better grip and made possible much more precise manipulation of objects.

organism: a plant or animal body; an organized group of cells in which different groups of cells do different jobs for the whole body's survival. (This word can also refer to all living things, including one-celled life.)

ozone: (*o*-zon) a gas made of oxygen atoms hooking together in groups of three (regular atmospheric—free—oxygen is in groups of two atoms); a layer of ozone floats about 30 miles above the Earth's surface and is very important to life, since it filters out most of the harmful ultraviolet rays of the sun.

Pangaea: (pan-*gee*-a) the name given by scientists to the one supercontinent that existed before forces inside the Earth created several smaller continents.

photosynthesis: (fo-to-*sin*-thuh-sis) from the Latin words meaning "to make something out of light"; this is the process in which plant cells soak up sunlight, carbon dioxide, and water, to make protein, their food.

planets: heavenly bodies in orbit around a star; they do not themselves give off light, but reflect the light of their local star.

predators: (*pred*-uh-tawrz) animals that feed on other animals.

primate: a kind of mammal, initially and/or presently tree-dwelling (such as the chimpanzee, gorilla, etc.), that has stereoscopic eyes, skillful hands, opposable thumbs, and a highly developed brain.

protein: very complex molecules made of many different amino acids; most living things are made of protein (among other chemicals), and all animals have to eat protein to stay alive.

protocells: (*pro*-to-selz) tiny microspheres containing many of the necessary ingredients to becoming living cells, but not having the ability to split into exact copies of the original cell and pass the message along to future generations.

proton: one of the basic particles that make up atoms; protons are found in the center of all atoms.

radiation: one of the powerful but invisible forms of energy that comes out of stars and other high-energy sources; radiation consists of tiny particles speeding through space.

radioactivity: a form of radiation that comes out of certain kinds of rocks, including uranium and plutonium.

***Ramapithecus*:** (*Rah*-muh-pi-*thee*-kus) a ground-dwelling descendant of the earliest primates, which scientists think was our direct ancestor; *Ramapithecus* lived on the ground about 15 million years ago in several parts of the world where primates were forced out of the trees by the changing climatic conditions that thinned out jungles and forests.

Renaissance: (*Ren*-uh-sahns) the period of revival of much classical knowledge and art in western European countries from the 14th to the 16th centuries A.D.

replicator: (*rep*-li-kay-tawr) a cell that can split into two exact copies of itself and pass along the message to grow, split, and continue the process into future generations; the key ingredient in replicating cells is the supermolecule DNA.

reptile: a kind of animal that evolved from a branch of the amphibians and was adapted for survival on dry land in hot climates; some branches of the reptile family evolved to live in water, in the air, and on land; lizards, turtles, snakes, and dinosaurs are reptiles.

rickets: a disease from insufficient vitamin D; rickets weakens bones and causes females to die in childbirth.

scientific method: the building of conclusions from experiments and direct observation; scientists who use the scientific method are willing to let their experiments be done by other scientists to see if they get the same results.

scientists: the men and women who work in the different branches of science covered in this book: astronomers, chemists, physicists, astrophysicists, geologists, anthropologists, archeologists, paleoanthropologists, sociologists, psychologists, biochemists, biophysicists, biologists, molecular biologists, and many more.

scorpion: a small crablike invertebrate.

sea urchin: an underwater animal that protects itself by having long sharp spines sticking outward.

social animal: animal that instinctively lives in groups; early primates, hominids, and humans were and are social animals, as are some other mammals, insects, and birds.

social selection: the process by which humans mate more frequently with those in the group who are considered more attractive, leading to the spread of those people's traits in the group. This has the effect of selecting certain characteristics and suppressing others within each group of humans.

species: (*spee*-sheez) a group of closely related living things that can reproduce with each other.

sperm: male sex cells capable of movement by means of flagella attached to the outside; each sperm cell contains a single strand of the animal's DNA, and can hook together with a female (egg) cell's single strand to begin the growth of a new organism.

stars: burning fireballs in which hydrogen is fused into helium (and in large stars into heavier atoms).

stereoscopic eyes: (*ster*-ee-o-scahp-ik) a pair of eyes that both point forward; having stereoscopic eyes gives better depth perception than those whose eyes are more on the sides of their heads.

stromatolite: (stro-*mat*-uh-lyt) a mat made of millions upon millions of algae cells growing together in a colony in the water; scientists have found the dried-up and hardened remains of some of these mats and think they grew at least 2 billion years ago.

subspecies: a group within a species that has different characteristics from the rest of the members of the species but can still interbreed with them.

sun: the star at the center of our solar system; not a massive star, our sun has probably been burning for 5 billion years and has about another 5 billion years to go.

supernova: (*syoo*-per-no-vuh) the explosion of a large star after it has used up all its hydrogen atoms and collapsed inward; in the extremely intense heat and pressure of a supernova, heavier atoms are formed and thrown out into the galaxy along with the atoms that were formed during the star's life.

Technological Revolution: the enormous change in industrialized countries brought about by a series of inventions including electricity, computers, telephones, jet planes, television, nuclear energy, etc.

tides: the rising and falling of water in the Earth's ocean and lakes due to the gravitational pull of the moon as it passes.

trilobite: (*try*-luh-byt) a primitive invertebrate that flourished in the ocean millions of years ago and eventually became extinct.

ultraviolet light: part of the spectrum of the light that comes from stars; ultraviolet light is very destructive to life and causes mutations in living cells, but fortunately most of our sun's ultraviolet light is filtered out by the ozone layer above the Earth's surface.

uterus: (*yoot*-er-uhs) the area in a female mammal's abdomen where fertilized egg cells grow into offspring ready for birth.

vertebrates: (*vuhr*-tuh-bruhts) animals with backbones and skeletons inside their bodies; fish, reptiles, and humans are vertebrates.

vitamin D: a substance vital to human health; we can manufacture vitamin D from sunlight shining on our skin or get it from eating foods that contain it (fish, milk, and others); if humans don't get enough vitamin D, they get rickets, a disease that weakens bones and causes mothers to die in childbirth.

volcano: a mountain formed by hardened lava when a crack opens in the Earth's crust and molten lava surges to the surface.

warm-blooded: in animals, having the ability to keep the body temperature almost the same even when the outside temperature goes up or down; warm-bloodedness works by the chemical "burning" of food inside the body, which generates heat from within; warm-blooded animals (mammals and birds) keep much of this heat in by the insulation of fur and feathers.

white dwarfs: what small stars become after they have burned up all their hydrogen atoms and collapsed inward; white dwarfs give off very little energy.

Summary

Here is a shortened list of the events from the beginning of our universe to the present moment:

- the Big Bang occurs
- hydrogen and helium atoms are formed and swirl into clouds
- the first stars begin to burn
- fusion produces bigger atoms inside some stars
- the biggest stars explode (supernovas) and scatter their atoms
- new stars form, among them our sun
- the planet Earth is formed
- the Earth's core melts and volcanoes spew out lava and gases
- atoms hook into molecules on the Earth's surface
- the Earth cools down, clouds form, and it begins to rain
- many years of rainfall form the Earth's oceans, lakes, etc.
- amino acids and nucleotide bases form and dissolve in the water
- protocells are formed in the water
- the first living cells begin splitting in two and passing the message of life along
- mutations produce a variety of living cells; the well adapted survive
- bacteria cells evolve, eating other cells
- green algae cells evolve, using sunlight to make protein
- oxygen from the algae cells changes life underwater

- oxygen begins to fill up the atmosphere above the Earth's surface
- an ozone layer forms and filters out most ultraviolet rays of the sun
- modern eucaryotic plant and animal cells evolve
- sexual reproduction begins among some cells, adding to diversity
- some cells begin to live in large colonies
- the first plant and animal organisms evolve
- the first fish evolve
- some plants begin to grow on dry land
- some invertebrates begin to crawl onto dry land
- amphibians spend part of their time on dry land
- the Earth's land masses are pushed together into one continent, Pangaea
- the Earth's climate gets hotter and drier and many swamps dry out
- reptiles emerge as the dominant animal on land
- birds and mammals evolve from branches of the reptile family
- Pangaea begins to break up into several smaller continents
- 65 million years ago, all dinosaurs suddenly become extinct
- mammals emerge as the dominant land animal
- some small mammals begin to live in the trees
- primates evolve with bodies completely adapted to tree dwelling
- continents collide, throwing up mountains and changing climates
- many thick jungles thin out to open grasslands
- primates are forced to retreat to the remaining jungles
- the primates of East Africa are trapped and must live on the ground
- some land-dwelling primates survive and evolve into hominids

- some hominids evolve with upright posture, better brains, an omnivorous diet, and stone tools and weapons
- some hominids live in temporary camps, sharing the food they hunt and gather and passing along ideas by language
- some hominids evolve with larger brains and bodies and spread into Asia and Europe
- hominids learn how to control fire and cook food
- *Homo sapiens sapiens* (modern humans) evolves
- agriculture is invented and the idea spreads rapidly
- humans begin to live in villages, towns, and cities
- human civilization grows—laws, religions, art, etc.
- empires battle each other for territory and modern nations are formed
- the Renaissance in Europe begins
- the Industrial Revolution changes Western life
- the Technological Revolution brings great promise, but also dire threats
- you are born

Imagine that the life of the universe could be laid out along 100 yards (the length of a football field). At one end is the Big Bang, and at the other end is now. On this scale, each yard is 150 million years. This is where a few important events are located:

Yard 0	The Big Bang
Yard 70	The formation of the Earth
Yard 77	The first living cells
Yard 97	The first fish
Yard 99	Dinosaurs on the Earth
Yard 100	Now

As you can see, a lot is squeezed into that 100th yard—the evolution of mammals, primates, hominids, and finally humans.

In fact, *Homo sapiens sapiens* evolved in the last hundredth of an inch—a tiny sliver of time in the life of the universe. We humans are pretty recent arrivals.

Bibliography

Allison, Linda. *The Reasons for the Seasons.* Boston: Little, Brown & Co., 1975

Asimov, Isaac. *What Makes the Sun Shine?* Boston: Atlantic Monthly Press (Little, Brown & Co.), 1971

Beadle, George W. and Muriel. *The Language of Life.* New York: Anchor Press (Doubleday & Co., Inc.), 1966

Bergamini, David, and the Editors of *Life. The Universe.* Boston: Time-Life Books (Time, Inc.), 1969

Boeke, Kees. *Cosmic View: The Universe in 40 Jumps.* New York: John Day Co., Inc., 1957

Bronowski, Jacob. *The Ascent of Man.* Boston: Little, Brown & Co., 1974

Burton, Virginia Lee. *Life Story.* Boston: Houghton Mifflin Co., 1962

Cairns, Trevor, ed. *Cambridge Introduction to the History of Mankind.* New York: Cambridge University Press, 1969

Calder, Nigel. *The Life Game.* New York: The Viking Press, Inc., 1974

Cohen, Robert. *The Color of Man.* New York: Random House, Inc., 1968

Cudmore, L. Larison. *The Center of Life.* New York: Quadrangle/The New York Times Co., 1977

Dawkins, Richard. *The Selfish Gene.* New York: Oxford University Press, Inc., 1976

Eiseley, Loren. *The Immense Journey.* New York: Vintage Books (Random House, Inc.), 1957

Encyclopaedia Britannica Macropaedia, vol. 10, 1978. "Life" (by Carl Sagan).

Fahs, Sophia Lyon, and Spoerl, Dorothy T. *Beginnings: Earth, Sky, Life, Death.* Boston: Beacon Press, Inc., 1958

Folsome, Clair Edwin, ed. *The Origin of Life.* San Francisco: W. H. Freeman & Co., 1979

Gale, Ramona-Ann. *Prehistoric Life.* New York: Grosset & Dunlap, Inc., 1976

Gordon, Patrick. *The Unfolding Past.* New York: Oxford University Press, 1974

Gould, Stephen Jay. *Ever Since Darwin.* New York: W. W. Norton & Co., Inc., 1977

Hessel, Milton. *Man's Journey Through Time.* New York: Wanderer Books (Simon & Schuster, Inc.), 1974

Holmes, Edward. *Know About the World.* New York: Golden Press (Western Publishing Co., Inc.), 1972

Jastrow, Robert. *Until the Sun Dies.* New York: W. W. Norton & Co., Inc., 1977

Lancaster, Jane B. "Carrying and Sharing in Human Evolution." *Human Nature,* February 1978

Leakey, Richard, and Lewin, Roger. *Origins.* New York: E. P. Dutton & Co., Inc., 1977

Leakey, Richard, and Lewin, Roger. "Origins of the Mind." *Psychology Today,* July 1978

Leutscher, Alfred. *Dinosaurs and Other Ancient Reptiles and Mammals.* New York: Grosset & Dunlap, Inc., 1975

Macdonald, Malcolm Ross. *The Origin of Johnny.* New York: Alfred A. Knopf (Random House, Inc.), 1975

McGowan, Tom. *Album of Prehistoric Man.* Chicago: Rand McNally & Co., 1975

Motz, Lloyd. *The Universe.* New York: Charles Scribner's Sons, 1976

Reader's Digest Association. *The Last Two Million Years.* New York: Reader's Digest Press, 1974

Rhodes, Frank T. *Evolution.* New York: Golden Press (Western Publishing Co., Inc.), 1974

Sagan, Carl. *Broca's Brain.* New York: Random House, Inc., 1979

Sagan, Carl. *The Dragons of Eden.* New York: Random House, Inc., 1977

Shklovskii, I. S., and Sagan, Carl. *Intelligent Life in the Universe.* New York: Delta Books (Dell Publishing Co., Inc.), 1966

Scientific American, Editors of. *Evolution.* San Francisco: W. H. Freeman & Co., 1978

Scientific American, Editors of. *Life, Origins, and Evolution.* San Francisco: W. H. Freeman & Co., 1978

Sullivan, Walter. *Continents in Motion.* New York: McGraw-Hill Book Co., 1974

Wallechinsky, David, and Wallace, Irving. *The People's Almanac.* New York: Doubleday & Co., Inc., 1975

Index